MW00789310

simple meals &
fabulous feasts from Italy

tuscany

Katie & Giancarlo
Caldesi

Other books by Katie & Giancarlo Caldesi:

The Amalfi Coast: A Collection of Italian Recipes
Venice: Recipes Lost and Found
Rome: Centuries in an Italian Kitchen
Sicily: Recipes from an Italian Island

recipe notes

— Unless otherwise stated: all fruit and vegetables are medium-sized; all fruit and herbs are fresh; all eggs are free-range and medium-sized.

— All olive oil used in this book is extra-virgin olive oil.

— Raw or lightly cooked eggs should be avoided by pregnant women, the elderly and very young children.

— Recipes that contain nuts should be avoided by those with a known allergic reaction to nuts and nut derivatives.

— Oven temperature: these are given for fan ovens. If you are using a conventional oven, increase the heat by around 20°C (50°F). You can also check with the manufacturer's handbook.

PHOTOGRAPHY
BY HELEN CATHCART

simple meals &
fabulous feasts from Italy

tuscany

**Katie & Giancarlo
Caldesi**

hardie grant books

contents

Tuscany is a region of the soul... it is impossible to reduce it to a geographical place. Tuscany is rather felt, found, recognised, lived & inevitably loved.

–

**Andrea Bocelli
(Italian singer/songwriter)**

introduction

The Italians have the phrase *'ben curato'*, meaning 'well cared for'; Tuscany is *ben curato*. On my first visit to this green and pleasant, fertile land I was mesmerised by the neat fields – every hill and valley had some edible crop growing on it. It looked as though a giant hand, perhaps belonging to an old Etruscan god, had reached down and combed each field neatly into place. The thoughtful being had placed a perfectly sized town on top of each hill and drawn a little winding road with his finger up to each one. It is this order, the friendly and welcoming landscape that Tuscany possesses, that has attracted so many of us, over millennia, to visit and fall in love with this region. It is about the size of Wales, inhabited by just under 3.8 million people, yet more than 40 million tourists visit every year.

We have travelled all over Tuscany for the last 20 years, as it is Giancarlo's homeland. He was born and raised in Montepulciano Stazione, a tiny village near the Umbrian border. He remembers a happy yet tough childhood living on his family smallholding, helping his mother with the cooking and his father on the land. They had little money and mostly ate what they grew. Marietta was Giancarlo's mother; sadly she was very ill when I met her. I would have relished learning from her first-hand and often imagine I hear her whispering advice in my ear. I am fascinated by the way she, and her mother before her, used to cook. Both cooked over an open fire using a grill positioned over the embers and had a tripod for a cauldron (which we still have) for one-pot dishes. Baking happened once a fortnight in the outdoor oven.

Pre-1950s, life in Italy hadn't changed for generations, and I believe old Tuscan cooking (with some exceptions) was healthier than it is now. Everything the Caldesi family ate was organic, seasonal and fresh. And that was the norm. I want to adopt all Marietta's ideas of fresh home cooking – the lovely herb-filled Tuscan dishes, the slow-cooked meat stews, the hearty soups and the light, just-picked salads – but I want to translate them for today's cooks. When Giancarlo talked about how his mother ran her kitchen, we thought this might not be possible today, but in fact it seems increasingly relevant as we become more conscious of what we eat and what we waste. Marietta's food is what we should be eating now: good food cooked from scratch, from field to fork.

Post 1950s, motorcars, fridges and pesticides came in, sugar and dried pasta became widely available, flour was imported and women went to work. Believe me, although I love cooking, I don't want to be tied to a kitchen sink or a hot oven seven days a week, as Marietta was, and today many of our younger Italian friends of both sexes follow a career path outside the home. However, what many Tuscans still want is good home cooking. According to a study by Unioncamere, Italy's chamber of commerce, the financial crisis and soaring unemployment have forced Italians to spend less and shop more cautiously, replacing fizzy drinks and sugary snacks with homemade produce. Half of Italians now buy 'only the essentials', according to the survey, and what they do buy is carefully chosen, with many buying directly from small producers and markets.

Living the Tuscan dream – going back to the land

Around 15 per cent of Italians grow their own food and 17 per cent of these started in the last five years, coinciding with the financial downturn. Combined with the economic benefits of growing your own, Italians are increasingly worried about the quality and purity of food. The phrase *cibo genuino* crops up again and again, and Tuscans tell me that they want 'natural food' that is uncontaminated with chemicals. The organic aisle in the Tuscan supermarket stretches far further than in my local supermarket in the UK. Biodynamic and organic wines are readily available, too.

There is something elemental about planting a seed, watching the plants develop and tasting the ripe fruit. It seems to me that Tuscans have never been as disconnected with the production of food as we have become. From medieval times to the present, Tuscan cuisine, just like the Etruscan cuisine before it (see page 16), is tied to the agriculture of the area. The real wine movement in the UK and the farm to table trend in the US seem quite new to us but the Tuscans have been growing, buying and cooking food in this way for generations. Our friend Fabrizio Biagi thinks we should all be 'moving towards the future with the methods of the past'. He gave us an example: his friend catches fresh anchovies at night by lamplight in Viareggio. He gives them to Fabrizio who preserves them in jars under salt, and he in turn gives some jars back to his friend. Fabrizio then uses them (we ate one on thickly buttered bread – heaven) and each time he opens the jar he has a connection, a relationship with that food and its origin, and knows every ingredient in it.

Many Tuscan families still have an *orto* – an area for growing food – whether it is outside the back door or on an allotment. There is a small but burgeoning movement of people choosing to grow in an *orto sinergico*, meaning to grow in synergy with the natural rhythms of the world. Our friends Livia and Nello, now in their seventies, have always farmed like this. Far from being a little cuckoo, it is a holistic approach that harnesses the power of nature by farming in harmony with insects, using mixed planting between flowers and vegetables and sowing according to the phases of the moon, the *ciclo lunare*, to help plants thrive. Even our friends' local town newspaper suggests when it is best to cut your hair or when to plant seeds according to the phases of the moon. In towns where Tuscans can't grow their own food, there are an increasing number of 'zero kilometre' restaurants specialising in locally sourced produce.

To ensure the quality of the food they put into their bodies, Italians are prepared to spend 14.4 per cent of their income on food compared to 8.9 per cent in the UK. They are also prepared to spend the time gathering ingredients. On a recent visit to Siena, our friend Antonella Rossi pointed out of the window and told me where all her ingredients were from. She grew the vegetables in her *orto*, the chillies were from a pot outside her front door, her olive oil was made from olives on the trees outside her window and the pigeons for the ragù came from the farm down the road. While she was telling me this I was wondering what I would have to say to a friend who came over for supper – 'This is from this supermarket,' 'This I got online,' and 'This is from the local corner shop.' I know I couldn't name the exact provenance of most of my food.

Antonella and her husband Fabrizio took us to buy cheese and salami for Christmas direct from the producers. They live on a budget but none of the food they bought was a bargain – that wasn't the point. They weren't trying to save pennies; they wanted to ensure they bought safe and good-quality food. Again, I couldn't imagine doing this back home. Here, in general, we seem more preoccupied with bargains than quality.

It might seem like I am looking at Tuscany with rose-tinted glasses, that we have formed an idealised view of Tuscan life and that we are not giving the real impression of Tuscany today. It is true that obesity is on the rise, as is diabetes (particularly in children), and I know some people in towns are hurriedly buying a panino for lunch and a ready meal for supper, but the numbers are less than in the UK and the US. And we are interested in those that are still living as people have done in Tuscany for thousands of years; those that are in pursuit of a good meal. We want to capture what we thought was special about Tuscany. To do this we have worked with family, friends and chefs who are passionate about their food and land. In Italy, someone like this who appreciates good food is called a *buona forchetta* – 'a good fork' – and happily Tuscany is full of them!

Twenty years ago when Giancarlo decided to specialise in Tuscan food, Giuliano Pacini was the first person he turned to. Having left Italy at such a young age, Giancarlo wanted to be reminded of his culinary roots. Giuliano, chef patron of Buca di Sant'Antonio in Lucca, was the perfect person to guide him through the finer points of Tuscan cooking and he is forever grateful for their long friendship (see picture opposite).

The collective pride

Everyone recognises Tuscany, the landscape punctuated by winding roads and pointed cypress trees; its clichéd images have graced tea trays, greetings cards and coasters for years. However, real people live, work and eat there! At the heart of every Tuscan there is a pride in their region, and an incredible sense of responsibility and love for their surroundings, their customs, recipes, their football teams and their wine. During the Renaissance, Boccaccio, the 14th century writer, wrote in *The Decameron* of the civic pride that he has in his own city, Florence, where he praised the qualities of Florentine men as 'noble, chivalrous, agreeable and wise' and the women 'all of whom are beautiful'. This fierce love of home is called *campanilismo*, which comes from the Italian word for bell tower – *campanile* – due to your home being defined by living close to the parish church bell.

Tuscans feel the need to celebrate what they have and show off, much to our benefit. The biannual *Palio di Siena*, for example, is the horse race around the fan-shaped Piazza del Campo in Siena. The Sienese compete with each other within their own city as they are divided into *contrade* (districts of the city). Each horse is taken into the local church to be blessed before the race, the area is decorated with the *contrade* flags and dinners are thrown in honour of the ancient race. The Sienese are happier when their rivals lose, rather than when their *contrade* wins, so fierce is the rivalry. The *Palio* replaced an earlier 'game' known as the *Gioca del Pugno* that took place in the Campo, which was a glorified fist fight between two *contrade* with 300 men on each team. Another example is the *sagre*, which are food festivals put on to celebrate the seasonal arrival of a particular food; you might have the *sagra* of the chestnuts, the new olive oil or the porchetta. It's taken very seriously and attended by all around.

'Just wait, be patient... Turn the heat to low and let the flavours develop.'

—

Antonella Secciani, Tuscan chef

The slow Tuscan life – how to make food taste Tuscan

The rhythm of life in Tuscany is slower than in Rome or the northern cities but faster than in Sicily, and many people visit or move here just for this pace. And the way Tuscans cook is also slower and calmer. In lessons from Tuscan chef Antonella Secciani, I learnt to slow down even more. 'Just wait, be patient,' she told me as we made a ragù. 'Turn the heat to low and let the flavours develop.' She showed me the level of heat over which the ragù should be made. The surface should merely 'quiver or tremble' in the pot. This will reduce the sauce, concentrating the flavour to the ultimate umami experience that gathers in the bottom of the pan waiting for a piece of meat or bread to scrape up the intense flavour. This is Tuscan cooking. She doesn't recommend putting the pan in the oven, using a slow cooker or a pressure cooker; the flavour won't develop in the same way.

In the chapter Skills from the Tuscan Kitchen (see page 23), we share the skills and tips we have learnt over the years for making food really taste Tuscan. It reflects how Marietta ran her kitchen where she made pasta, stock, tomato sauce and ragù, preserved fruits, dried herbs and cooked beans. The Tuscan kitchen is a frugal one and many of the recipes in this book cost very little to make. These kitchen skills are as relevant today as they ever were, and should never have fallen out of fashion.

Fat-bellied Etruscans who liked to party

The first settlers to make an impact on this region of Italy were the Etruscans. Their origin is debated – they could have been voyagers who came via the Eastern Mediterranean from Anatolia (also called Asia Minor). The earliest evidence of the Etruscans in Italy is found on the island of Elba, part of the Tuscan archipelago, and dates back to the 9th century BC. They formed Etruria and built hilltop towns such as Volterra, Cortona and Chiusi.

Their culture was heavily influenced by Greek society, with dining and drinking being favourite pastimes (to judge from their tomb paintings), so much so that the Romans condemned the Etruscans for their luxurious lifestyle and for allowing wives to take part in banquets.

We don't have any written evidence of recipes but they did leave pots, amphorae and plates behind, along with wall paintings in tombs depicting partying men and women who had fat bellies and glasses of wine to hand. It was one of the few societies where women seemed to be treated as equals and allowed to drink and party with the men. They liked to hunt, fish, grow and farm. They cooked over fires and used cauldrons just like Giancarlo's mother.

It is thanks to them that ingredients such as olive oil, herbs, chestnut flour, pulses, cereal such as barley, wild and sown vegetables, cheese, fish, wine and honey became widely used in Tuscan cuisine. They made farro soup, ate wild boar and pork and – like today – used every part of the pig. It is said that they dried the first ham and made the first prosciutto, and turned the first pork bellies into porchetta. They ate beef from the famous white Chianina cattle.

Etruscan Tuscany was seized by Rome in 351 BC. The last town to fall to the Romans was Cortona and eventually Etrurian Latin eclipsed the Etruscan language. City states were established and new cities at Lucca, Pisa, Siena and Florence were developed, the latter being established as a town for retired veterans from the Roman army. The Roman Empire collapsed in the 5th century AD, a fall partly brought about by Barbarian invasions.

Tuscany in the Middle Ages and why it looks like it does

During this time there was a form of sharecropping known as the *mezzadria*, with the wealthy landowner (the *padrone*) providing the land, house, some equipment and livestock to the tenants (*mezzadri*), who provided the labour (from an entire family). It is a system that is said to date back to Roman times.

The *mezzadria* was a version of the feudal system similar to our own in the UK, which died out centuries ago. In Tuscany, it was not abolished until the 1960s. We visited a *casa colonica*, a large detached house on a farm where families, sometimes up to 10 in each one, used to live in one large room and share a bathroom. It seemed an awful way to live and so recent you could still see the 1960s tiling and paint.

The families grew vegetables, wheat, and grapes for wine, made olive oil, had chickens, cows for milk and cheese, and other animals. Although the word *mezzadria*, which strictly translated means 'halving', implies that each party was entitled to 50 per cent of the annual production, in reality, after the church took its share and the *padrone* got his, the *mezzadri* were left with almost nothing. There are dishes like *strozzapreti*, meaning 'priest-stranglers', which illustrate the tenants' hatred of them. This dish was homemade gnocchi given to priests when they turned up, as you had to feed them regardless. The *mezzadri* did not have any protection or rights. You could benefit from a kind *padrone* or suffer at the hands of a cruel one, and they had the power to eject a family from their home with nothing. Many families nearly starved and were always worried about having enough to eat.

However, the *mezzadria* system is the very reason the Tuscan landscape changed from impenetrable thick woodland to neat, easily accessible vineyards and ploughed fields. Where you couldn't grow a crop you could graze animals, and the system provided the workers with the materials to make it happen. When the system was abolished people were free to go to work in the towns, and many farms and their *casa colonica* were abandoned.

Cucina povera

As well as being responsible for the changes to the landscape, the poverty resulting from the *mezzadria* system gave us a legacy of recipes which we now label as *cucina povera* – 'cooking of the poor'. During the Middle Ages, the diet of the average peasant was bread, or porridge-like soups made from a mixture of grains and dried beans. The soups were known as *puls* and it is from here we get the word 'pulse' for a legume. Meat was broken up and eaten with your fingers; at best there was a spoon for the juices or gruel-like thick soups. The food hasn't changed that much, except that people can afford to eat meat more often, fresh fish is more readily available and they have learnt to use a fork. (Apart from my husband that is, who still insists on eating dishes such as Rabbit in White Wine (see page 199) with his fingers and loves his soup thick. You can take the man out of Tuscany but you can't take Tuscany out of the man!) The Tuscans are still known by their Italian counterparts as the *mangiafagioli* ('beaneaters') for their love of beans. In fact, there are over 30 types of beans, also known as poor man's protein, that still feature in the Tuscan diet.

The lack of food was excused by the church during Lent, when the fast was a necessity as well as a religious event by virtue of the fact that in most years reserves of grain had been exhausted by this time. However, medieval cookbooks indicate that the nobility continued to enjoy a luxurious menu even during Lent, when the definition of 'fish' was extended to include whale, dolphin, beaver's tail and barnacle goose. In the 14th century the Anonimo Toscano, an anonymous Tuscan chef, wrote a book entitled *Libro dello Cocina*. In it he writes of the use of spices such as ginger, cloves, nutmeg, saffron and pepper, which were used to display wealth in the affluent homes of the day. We have included his version of a frittata made with wild herbs, known as *erbolata*, on page 86, as well as his recipe for cabbage and fennel cooked with saffron on page 234.

Cucina nobile – the Renaissance trendsetters

The other contrasting strand of Tuscan cooking is *cucina nobile* – the 'noble kitchen'. The growth and expansion of the wealthy Tuscan city-states through commerce, trade and agriculture led the mini-republics to find themselves frequently in conflict with one another. They had their own customs, dialects, differing ingredients and traditional recipes. At the same time there was substantial investment in art, culture and architecture, reaching a zenith in Florence during the rule of Lorenzo the Magnificent (1469–92). By 1435 Florence had expanded to take in nearly the whole of Tuscany except for Siena and Lucca.

Cuisine and eating habits formed during the Renaissance in Italy were the beginnings of the modern concept of Italian food and dining. Wealthy families such as the Medici in Florence and the Petrucci in Siena broke away from the eating traditions of the old and formed the basis for modern gourmet creations, incorporating new ingredients such as potatoes and peppers alongside the use of a novel utensil called the fork. Forks were first seen in Italy during a visit by an 11th century Byzantine princess to Venice and their use was in first instance frowned upon by the Church. They thought it a slight against God to not use the natural forks (our fingers) that he provided us with. When she died two years later they saw it as God's punishment for her vanity and pride. Centuries later the fork was finally accepted. Food was consumed from fine porcelain china at cloth-covered tables decorated with flowers as seen in the painting of The Last Supper by Leonardo da Vinci, rather than eaten off planks of wood. The Florentine palate was surprisingly sophisticated and it was during the 16th century that Buontalenti invented the custard-based gelato in Florence.

There are many myths surrounding Lorenzo the Magnificent's daughter Catherine de' Medici, who in 1533 – at the age of 14 – moved to France to marry the future King of France, Henry II. With her she took Florentine chefs, gardeners and vintners, and this is said to have changed French cuisine with the introduction of sauces such as *besciamella*, which became béchamel. She could well have encouraged the use of Tuscan ingredients as well as those from the New World and the use of the fork. In 1754, the *Encyclopédie* described French haute cuisine as 'decadent and effeminate', and explained that 'fussy sauces and fancy fricassees' arrived in France via 'that crowd of corrupt Italians who served at the court of Catherine de' Medici'.

Our Tuscan inspiration

During the Middle Ages there was almost constant warfare between neighbouring city-states with regular battles between Florence and Pisa, and between Florence and Siena.

Even today, every Tuscan is vociferous in their loyalty to their home city, town or village, and battles are still fought on the football pitches and other sporting arenas. You can ask a person from the Maremma in the south of Tuscany about farro and they look blankly at you, but for the Lucchese in the north it is a staple food. Our cousin from Buonconvento in the east thought very little of food between Volterra and Pisa – he told us not to even bother going there, and that 'real' Tuscan food was to be found near Arrezzo and Florence! This is why recipes have stayed so local, with no migration of ideas or ingredients from one province to another.

We decided to ignore our cousin's advice and have taken recipes from the entire region. I hope we have also managed to convey some of the Tuscan passion for what they have or what they are about to eat. From the minute they look out of their windows in the morning to the last nightcap at the bar, Tuscans, like most Italians, are immersed in food, and the chapters of this book take a culinary journey through a Tuscan day.

In all of our cookbooks about the Italian regions I begin by summing up the fundamental ingredients and principals: in *Amalfi* it was first catch your fish; in *Venice* it was first grind your spices in a pestle and mortar; in *Rome* it was grow your chilli and rosemary; in *Sicily* it was find lemons and oranges with leaves to ensure their freshness. And now, for *Tuscany*, my advice would be: don't rush, take your time… Know the provenance of your beef, tomatoes and wine, and let the ragù tremble over the lowest heat for as long as you can. It might even taste better the next day.

skills from the tuscan kitchen

skills from the tuscan kitchen

Do read this! These are the foundations of Tuscan cooking: the essential stocks, sauces and flavour bases. Master these and you can build your meals and really get the flavour of Tuscan food in your kitchen. I thought I knew a lot about Italian cooking, but I learnt so much more in the year of writing this book and concentrating on what made food Tuscan. This chapter is about passing on that knowledge we've acquired from working with our friends, family, and professional cooks from Tuscany such as Antonella Secciani, a cook at an *agriturismo* and restaurant. She is Tuscan through and through, and learnt to cook from her mother.

Giancarlo has immersed himself in the past and recalls the mantras and tips his mother, Marietta, his Auntie Agnese, and his neighbour Elide gave him as he would always be found in the kitchen with them. I often imagine hearing Marietta's voice in my ear telling me I haven't used enough olive oil, or haven't cooked something for long enough! 'Have patience,' she would have said. 'Give your body the good food and time it deserves.'

The Tuscan kitchen is a waste not, want not kitchen. During centuries of poverty nothing was thrown away. There was continuity in the kitchen: a stock used for two meals; tomato sauce used in several different ways; and leftovers respected and re-used (if it couldn't be eaten it went to the pigs, the chickens or back into the land). Everything was seasonal, freshly picked and eaten quickly as there were no fridges. People preserved food throughout the year, from gluts of fruit in summer to the pig slaughtered in winter. Now, as in the past, Tuscan locals tend to shop daily. This ensures fresh ingredients but also for many older people it is a ritual: a daily chore that provides contact with local people, a chance to talk, and the exercise of walking up a hill and down again. This is part of the Mediterranean life that keeps people healthy.

Giancarlo will always value the tips passed down from his Auntie Orlandina (bottom left), family friend Livia (top centre) and his mother Marietta Bellugi (top right)

olive oil

**ALWAYS BUY
EXTRA-VIRGIN
OLIVE OIL**

It's all about the oil! Olive trees form the landscape of Tuscany and their oil fuels the people who live on it; the same pure extra-virgin liquid gold that has been valued in Mediterranean cooking for millennia. These cultures usually have good health and longevity. We trust and love olive oil.

I remember standing in our friend's kitchen admiring an old tile – it was painted with an image of medieval peasants collecting olives from the trees. Out of the window that day I could hear a familiar sound and looked out to see the same image of men hard at work gathering olives, only this time with electric rakes. Nothing had changed in this eternal marriage between Italians and their beloved olive oil. This is the first lesson in Tuscan cooking. Don't try and cook Italian food with any other cooking oil; the flavour won't be the same.

Tuscan food has developed around their robust and peppery Tuscan oil. In the mountainous areas of northern Tuscany where olive trees can't be grown, pork fat is the main cooking fat.

Always buy extra-virgin olive oil. It is from the first pressing of the olives. It is the least processed and has to have less than 0.8 per cent free oleic acid. The lower this percentage of oleic acid, the higher the quality of the oil. It should have a fresh flavour of olives. Avoid olive oils that have been extracted with the aid of chemicals. A good-quality extra-virgin olive oil should be produced at a temperature below 30°C (86°F). If the temperature is higher it degrades the oil.

Check out the range of regional oils on offer in shops and delis and always bring some back if you travel in Italy. Price is a good indicator of quality. We buy one standard extra-virgin olive oil probably made from a blend of olives from Europe for cooking, and a more expensive single-estate oil from Italy for finishing food.

Extra-virgin olive oil loses its flavour over time. Every winter, new oil is made and this fresh oil is used where you can taste it the most: as a final flourish on tomato bruschetta; swirled into a warm soup; or drizzled over grilled meats, steamed vegetables or hot pasta, where the heat will warm up the oil and release the aroma of freshly pressed olives. Last year's oil can be used for everything else.

Olive oil does have a lower smoke point than nut, seed or coconut oil, but it is only a little lower. We use it for everything apart from deep-fat frying. (For more olive oil facts see caldesi.com.)

soffritto

THIS QUANTITY WORKS
FOR RECIPES THAT SERVE 4

75 g (2½ oz) carrot
   (1 medium carrot)
75 g (2½ oz) celery (1–2 stalks),
   with a few leaves if you
   have them
100 g (3½ oz) white onion
   (1 medium onion)
5 tablespoons extra-virgin
   olive oil
salt and freshly ground
   black pepper

THIS QUANTITY WORKS
FOR RECIPES THAT SERVE 6–8

150 g (5 oz) carrots
   (2–3 medium carrots)
150 g (5 oz) celery (2–3 stalks),
   with a few leaves if you
   have them
150 g (5 oz) white onion
   (1½ medium onions)
150 ml (5 fl oz/⅔ cup)
   extra-virgin olive oil
salt and freshly ground
   black pepper

OTHER OPTIONAL FLAVOURS

2 garlic cloves, peeled and
   lightly crushed (remove any
   green germinating core)
handful of parsley with soft
   stalks, finely chopped
2 large sprigs of rosemary
   and/or thyme, left whole
2 bay leaves, left whole
fresh chilli, finely chopped,
   or dried chilli flakes, to taste

This is the essential base flavour for nearly all Italian stews, soups, sauces and ragù. It is made from gently fried tiny cubes of celery, onion and carrot. Sometimes parsley or a couple of whole garlic cloves are chopped with it, and rosemary sprigs or chilli are added to the pan. You cannot hope to make Tuscan food without knowing how to make a good *soffritto*; it will add richness and umami flavours to the dish. Try to find the best and freshest vegetables – it does make a difference. A *soffritto* made with vegetables from the garden tastes infinitely better than one made from polytunnel-grown vegetables that have been travelling and stored for weeks. It is surprising to taste a carrot straight from the ground; it is so naturally sweet.

Do use enough oil or you will never be able to cook the onions and carrots for long enough to get the sweetness out of them without them burning.

Finely chop the carrot, celery, onion and parsley, if using, by hand or in a food processor (if you use the latter, make sure you don't end up with a paste).

Heat the oil in a large frying pan over a medium heat. Add the garlic, if using, and fry for 1 minute. Stir in the remaining ingredients including any optional flavours, if using, and season. Sweat the vegetables over a low heat, stirring and shaking the pan frequently, for 15–20 minutes or until the vegetables have softened. The colours will have changed from bright and sharp to soft and golden. Use the *soffritto* straight away or freeze it. It will keep in the freezer for up to 3 months – defrost before using.

poor man's ragù

We were shown this sauce of a reduced *soffritto* by Giancarlo's cousin, Tiziana Caldesi (see picture opposite). It is known as a 'lying sauce' as it is similar to a meat ragù and was made to dress pasta when there was no meat available. It is a good vegetarian option that we sometimes serve if we are having a ragù. Tiziana makes a standard *soffritto* for six people, adding a big handful of parsley, and chilli to taste (no pepper), then lets it sweat over a low heat for 30 minutes. Then she adds 400 g (14 oz) tomato passata from a jar and cooks it for a further 30 minutes. It is then used to coat freshly cooked and drained short pasta such as penne, and served with a sprinkling of finely grated Parmesan.

battuto

THIS QUANTITY WORKS FOR RECIPES THAT SERVE 6–8

4 garlic cloves, peeled
4 long sprigs of rosemary, leaves picked
handful of sage leaves
salt and freshly ground black pepper

This is a finely chopped mixture of flavours, or *aromi* as the Italians would call it. It is a savoury base used to flavour sauces, casseroles, fish, roast meats or simply dusted onto toasted bread with oil. The herbs are chopped finely together with garlic and seasoning before being added to olive oil in a pan. In mountainous regions where olive trees can't grow, pork fat is used for frying and this is chopped with the herbs to form a paste.

Cut the hard ends off the garlic. Use a large knife to coarsely chop the garlic, herbs and seasoning together into small dice the size of fine gravel.

stocks

Excellent and versatile stock should be made from things you would normally discard in the kitchen. I freeze vegetable peelings throughout the week, adding bendy carrots that have seen better days, celery ends and leaves, pepper cores, parsley stalks, tops and tails of onions and coarse, dark leek ends. I also do the same with raw and cooked chicken bones and carcasses, fish bones and prawn (shrimp) shells. I never bother defrosting the vegetables or meat – I just add them to the pot as they are.

The better the stock, the better the flavour of the final dish, and a natural flavour is infinitely better than a stock from a cube or powder. Make stocks when you are at home and not rushing about. They need time to bubble away gently and make the house smell like a home. Use them up a few days after making them, or reduce them to an intense, concentrated stock and freeze them in small batches ready for when you need them.

poached chicken & chicken stock

**MAKES APPROX. 3 LITRES
(5¼ PINTS/12¾ CUPS)
OF STOCK AND 650–700 G
(1 LB 7 OZ–1 LB 9 OZ)
COOKED MEAT**

1.5–2 kg (3 lb 5 oz–4 lb 6 oz)
  chicken (including giblets)
4 litres (7 pints/17 cups)
  cold water
1 medium white onion,
  unpeeled and roughly
  chopped, or large handful
  of onion peelings
2 celery stalks with leaves,
  roughly chopped
1 leek top or 6 spring onion
  (scallion) tops, roughly
  chopped (optional)
small handful of parsley stalks
  (optional)
1 medium carrot, roughly
  chopped, or large handful
  of carrot peelings
6 black peppercorns
1 Parmesan rind
3 cloves
2 bay leaves

**From one chicken you can make three meals: a delicate and nourishing
stock to use in a huge variety of other recipes, hot poached chicken
to eat straight away, and the leftover meat to keep in the fridge for
another meal. In Italy you can easily buy an old chicken that has passed
retirement age for egg laying. It will have been plucked and cleaned
but have the feet still intact (the birds are usually yellowish in colour
as they are corn fed). The old birds are tough and need a long cooking
time but have a better flavour than a young bird.**

**In the UK I can't easily get hold of an old bird so I buy a whole large
chicken with the giblets. The giblets are really important for a good
flavour in the stock. Once a week I poach a chicken with vegetables and
seasoning, taking the chicken out of the stock halfway through once its
cooked (unlike the Italian way, as my chicken isn't old so it doesn't need
as long as an old hen). I pick the meat off the carcass and put the bones
back into the stock to strengthen the flavour. I use the boiled skin to
make chicken crackling (see opposite). We eat the juicy poached meat
hot with salsa verde (see page 123), or I leave it to cool and make
salads, panini, meatloaf, risotto and soup. Nothing goes to waste.**

**If we use chicken thighs we buy ones with the bone in for more
flavour and the skin on to make chicken crackling.**

Put the chicken in a large stock pot with the water and add the remaining
ingredients. Bring to the boil then reduce the heat to a gentle simmer. Skim
the surface frequently to remove the foam, particularly at the beginning,
adding a little more water if the level becomes too low.

After about 1½ hours the bird will be cooked through: look for the moment
when the legs fall away easily from the carcass. Remove the chicken from the
stock with tongs, allowing any liquid to drain back into the pot, then put it on
a board to cool for 10–15 minutes. Removing the bird at this point means the
meat isn't overcooked but it has still given flavour to the stock. Once it's cool
enough to handle, pick the meat from the bones and put the bones back into
the pot to continue cooking for a further 1½ hours.

Strain the stock into a large, clean bowl, reserving any large pieces of
vegetables and the liver to eat cold or use in other recipes. Discard the
remaining peelings, flavourings, bones, giblets and cartilage. Use the stock
straight away or store in the fridge for up to 4 days or freeze for up to 3 months.
To save freezer space it is a good idea to cook the strained stock for up to an
hour longer to reduce it and concentrate its flavour.

Chicken stock from cooked bones

If I roast a chicken I save the fat to reuse for cooking (roast potatoes in chicken fat are delicious), and freeze the carcass and bones for a stock. Follow the recipe opposite using the carcasses and bones instead of a fresh chicken. Ideally you need 2–2.5 kg (4 lb 6 oz–5 lb 5 oz) of bones, so you will need more than one chicken. Cooked or raw bones can be frozen and then used to make stock.

Chicken crackling

Chicken crackling is a revelation and totally delicious. Stretch out pieces of skin onto a baking tray, scatter with a little salt, and cook for 20 minutes at 180°C (350°F/Gas 4) or until crisp. The skin can be crumbled onto a chicken salad or a chicken casserole, or served with chicken in a *panino*.

prawn stock

MAKES APPROX. 2 LITRES
(3½ PINTS/8½ CUPS)

3 tablespoons extra-virgin
    olive oil
1.5 kg (3 lb 5 oz) raw seafood
    shells and heads
1 medium carrot, halved
    lengthways, or large handful
    of carrot peelings
1 white onion, roughly
    chopped, or large handful
    of onion peelings
100 ml (3 ½ fl oz/scant ½ cup)
    white wine
3 litres (5¼ pints/12¾ cups)
    hot water

Any time we use shellfish such as crabs, prawns (shrimp), crayfish, langoustines and lobsters we buy them with their heads and shells so that we can keep them for making a stock. This broth adds a wonderful flavour to any seafood dish and no shop-bought stock compares to it. We use it for the farro soup on page 138, but you can also use it in seafood pasta dishes or in a fish sauce.

Heat the oil in a large stock pot over a medium heat. Add the seafood shells and heads with the carrot and onion. When the shells start to brown and stick to the bottom of the pan add the wine, increase the heat and let it reduce for 4–5 minutes. Bash the shells, particularly any prawn or lobster heads, with a wooden rolling pin to release the juices and break up the shells. Pour in the hot water, bring to the boil, then reduce the heat and simmer for 1–1½ hours. We don't skim this broth as you lose the flavour and the lovely orange colour by doing this. Remove from the heat. Strain the stock into a large jug or bowl, squeezing the juices from the shells by pressing down on them with a ladle. Discard the shells. Use the stock straight away or store in an airtight container in the fridge for up to 4 days. You can also simmer the stock for a further 30 minutes–1 hour to reduce it and then freeze for up to 3 months.

beef bone broth

MAKES APPROX. 1.4 LITRES
(2 PINTS/6 CUPS)

1 kg (2lb 3 oz) raw beef bones
    such as oxtail and shin of beef
5 litres (8¾ pints/12¾ cups)
    cold water
1 medium carrot, roughly
    chopped, or large handful
    of carrot peelings
1 large celery stalk, roughly
    chopped
½ large red onion, roughly
    chopped, or large handful
    of red onion peelings
2 large tomatoes, quartered
good handful of parsley stalks
1 fat garlic clove
2 cloves

This beefy broth is full of goodness and flavour from the bones. Antonella Rossi uses it for the Wood Pigeon Ragù on page 180. It can also be used to cook pasta or in a soup.

Preheat the oven to 220°C (425°F/Gas 7). Put the bones in a roasting tray and roast for 20 minutes. Carefully remove the bones from the tray, then put them in a large saucepan with the fresh cold water and the rest of the ingredients. Bring to the boil, then reduce the heat to low and simmer for 3 hours. Skim the surface frequently to remove any foam, adding a little more water if the level becomes too low.

Strain the stock into a large, clean jug or bowl, reserving any large pieces of vegetables to eat cold or use in other recipes. Discard the bones and other flavourings. Use the stock straight away or store in an airtight container in the fridge for up to 4 days, or freeze for up to 3 months. To save freezer space, simmer the strained stock for up to 1 hour longer to reduce it and concentrate its flavour.

pheasant stock

MAKES APPROX. 1.5 LITRES
(3 PINTS 3 FL OZ/6½ CUPS)

2 tablespoons extra-virgin
    olive oil
1 pheasant (with giblets if you
    have them)
1 white onion, roughly
    chopped, or large handful of
    onion peelings
1 carrot, roughly chopped, or
    the same weight in peelings
1 celery stalk (plus leaves if
    you have them), roughly
    chopped
8 juniper berries, roughly
    crushed
6 black peppercorns
5 parsley stalks (optional)
3 sprigs of thyme
1 bay leaf
200 ml (7 fl oz/generous ¾ cup)
    white wine
3 litres (102 fl oz/12¾ cups)
    hot water

Tuscany is a land of hunters who love to go out at weekends into the woods and shoot game. Roast game birds are notorious for being dry, but we find this way to cook them results in tender flesh and a tasty stock to boot. Other types of bird such as partridge can also be cooked in this way.

Heat the oil in a large stock pot over a medium heat. Add the pheasant, onion, carrot and celery, then fry, turning the pheasant until it is browned on all sides. Add the spices and herbs and stir. Pour in the wine and let it bubble over a medium heat for around 10 minutes, until it has evaporated. Add the hot water and let the pheasant simmer over a low heat for 1–1½ hours until the meat is tender and falls off the bone. Regularly skim the stock with a slotted spoon to remove any foam. When the meat is tender, remove the bird from the stock and put it on a board to cool for 10 minutes. Once cool enough to handle, pick the meat from the bones and use it for the risotto on page 112 or the soup on page 144, or eat it warm with the salsa verde on page 123. Put the bones back into the pot and cook over a low heat for a further 1½ hours.

Remove from the heat and strain the stock into a large jug or bowl. I like to use the carrot and celery in a soup or sauce – they seem too good to throw away. The stock can be used straight away or it will keep for up to 4 days in an airtight container in the fridge. Alternatively, freeze for up to 3 months.

vegetable stock

MAKES APPROX. 2 LITRES
(3½ PINTS/8½ CUPS)

2.2 litres (3¾ pints/9 cups)
    water
1 onion, roughly chopped,
    or a large handful of
    onion peelings
10 g (½ oz) parsley stalks
    (or leaves and stalks)
1 carrot, or the same weight
    in peelings, roughly chopped
leek ends, roughly chopped
1 celery stalk with a small
    handful of leaves
5 g (¼ oz) dried porcini
    mushrooms (optional)
1 Parmesan rind (optional)
1 bay leaf

A good vegetable stock makes use of leftovers and takes only 30 minutes to make. Instead of whole fresh vegetables, do use the peelings or vegetables past their best. The most important flavouring in my opinion is the celery leaves. Other enhancements are dried mushrooms or cheese rinds.

Put all the ingredients in a large stock pot, bring to the boil then reduce the heat and simmer for 30 minutes. Strain the stock into a large, clean bowl or jug, and reuse the vegetables for a minestrone if you wish. Simmer the strained stock for longer if you want a more concentrated stock for freezing. Use straight away, store in an airtight container in the fridge for up to 4 days. Alternatively, freeze for up to 3 months.

polenta

SERVES 6
(MAKES 24 SQUARES)

1 litre (34 fl oz/4¼ cups) water
 or stock, or 500 ml
 (17 fl oz/2¼ cups) whole
 (full-fat) milk and 500 ml
 (17 fl oz/2¼ cups) water for
 set polenta
150 g (5 oz/1 cup) polenta
10 g (½ oz) fine salt (or to taste)
plain (all-purpose) flour,
 for dusting (optional)
sunflower oil, for greasing
 and frying

**POLENTA
IS A GOOD
BASE FOR
GLUTEN-FREE
CROSTINI**

Polenta is ground dried maize. It can be yellow or white, and fine and smooth or rough and gritty. It has been a staple filling meal for centuries in Italy, more common in the north than the south. It can be eaten with savoury dishes or used in sweet cakes and biscuits. We like it served soft and made with plenty of butter and cheese. It forms a warm pillow for a rich ragù.

Giancarlo's father measured polenta by hand, letting a fistful (*manciata*) of polenta fall slowly into a pan of boiling, salted water from his hand held at head height, whisking it in as it fell. To cook polenta in milk was considered wasteful in his day, but we now recommend half milk and half water or vegetable stock for a richer finish.

Quick-cook polenta is used commonly in Italy and it is ready in just 5 minutes. There is a subtle difference in texture and flavour but only polenta aficionados would notice! If you do use quick-cook polenta, cook it following the packet instructions. Both set and soft polenta is made in the same way, but more liquid and a good dollop of butter is added to the soft version. Once polenta sets it becomes solid and can be cut into shapes and grilled or fried. It forms a good base for crostini toppings if you are following a gluten-free diet.

Bring the water, stock or milk/water mix to the boil in a large saucepan. Slowly pour the polenta from a height into the boiling water while stirring constantly for 5 minutes, then stir every 5 minutes for a further 35 minutes. Add the salt to taste and remove from the heat. Grease a shallow rectangular tin roughly 20 × 30 × 1.5 cm (8 × 12 × ¾ in) or a work surface with oil and pour the hot polenta onto it. Spread a little oil on top and flatten it down with an oiled spatula until it is 1.5 cm (¾ in) thick, then leave to cool until it is set firm. Cut the firm polenta into 24 squares, about 5 cm (2 in) in size. Toast the polenta squares under a grill until lightly browned. Alternatively, dip them in flour, shake off any excess, and fry in sunflower oil in a frying pan over a medium-high heat.

To make soft, cheesy polenta
Follow the recipe for set polenta but add a further 200 ml (7 fl oz/generous ¾ cup) water to the pan. Then stir in 100 g (3½ oz) butter and 50 g (2 oz) finely grated Parmesan at the end of cooking, for a rich flavour and glossy finish.

cooking greens

I have a theory that people who hate greens just haven't had them cooked by Italians! Tender cooked green leaves dressed with nothing but a slick of very good oil and a squeeze of lemon is our comfort food and a bowlful will be fought over at the kitchen table. Traditionally, Tuscans collected wild greens such as chicory, cress, nettle and dandelion leaves from the fields, which are used raw in a salad called a *misticanza* or cooked such as in the *erbolata* recipe on page 86. Depending on the time of year, the greens that are available vary, and each need to be treated differently. After cooking they can be finished according to the Sautéed Leaves with Chilli & Garlic recipe on page 227.

Weights of leaves

Leaves are typically sold with their stems intact, which weigh more than the leaves and you generally end up throwing them away. To end up with enough cooked leaves for a recipe you need to start with a lot of leaves!

Soft leaves such as spinach and Swiss chard, once stripped from their stems, usually cook down to half their raw weight. Tougher leaves such as cavolo nero or curly kale cook down to around two thirds of their raw weight once stripped on their stems depending on the density of the leaves.

How to prepare spinach

Baby spinach leaves should be washed and drained well. Then they need a mere flash of heat in the pan, stirred through with a little salt and extra-virgin olive oil. Larger leaves are best washed; then, without completely draining them, put them into a deep saucepan, cover and leave it to steam in the residual water with a little salt for 5–7 minutes until tender and wilted. Drain and leave to cool down. Squeeze the water out well, ideally with your hands.

How to prepare Swiss chard

Giancarlo's mother Marietta would never have thrown away the thick white or rainbow-coloured Swiss chard stems, but they do have a strong minerally flavour so they are not to everyone's taste. They have to be cooked separately to the leaves. Cut the stems from just under the leaf and chop them finely. Boil in salted water for 10–15 minutes, until tender. Prepare the leaves of Swiss chard as the larger spinach leaves above.

How to prepare cavolo nero

Pinch the rib around the middle of the leaf and pull the leaves away by running your fingers up and down the hard stalk. Discard the stalks. Wash the leaves under cold running water. Roughly shred the leaves and cook them in salted boiling water for up to 10 minutes, until soft and tender. Drain, then squeeze out the water when cool to the touch.

homemade tomato sauce

SERVES
4–6 PEOPLE

6 tablespoons extra-virgin olive oil
1 small red onion, peeled and finely chopped
2 garlic cloves, peeled and lightly crushed
1 teaspoon salt
freshly ground black pepper
2 × 400 g (14 oz) tins plum tomatoes (or 1 quantity passata – see opposite)

This is the tomato sauce that is essential to the Italian kitchen. A large jar or plastic box of it will be found in most Italian fridges. It is used on pasta, to give body to a casserole, to make Babbo's Eggs (see page 59), or to pep up a soup (I often purée it and serve it as a soup in itself). Don't skimp on the oil: if you don't use a generous amount you cannot cook the onions for long enough to get the sweetness out of them that balances the acidity of the tomatoes, and they would burn at the edges instead of sweating slowly and becoming translucent. Use an Italian brand of plum tomatoes – they usually taste better than from anywhere else – and always buy whole tomatoes instead of chopped, which can be watery. This sauce doesn't freeze brilliantly due to the water content but it will last up to five days in the fridge.

Heat the olive oil in a saucepan over a medium heat. Add the chopped onions and garlic, then season with salt and pepper. Cook for 5–7 minutes, stirring, until the onion has softened.

Add the tomatoes and crush them in the pan with a potato masher to break them up. Rinse each tin out with a ¼ tin of cold water and add this to the saucepan. Simmer over a low heat, uncovered, for about 40 minutes. Taste the sauce and adjust the seasoning as necessary.

•

Variation: Tomato soup

Blend the tomato sauce with a stick blender until smooth. Serve as a soup dressed with a swirl of good olive oil and a handful of grated Parmesan.

•

fresh tomato passata

MAKES APPROX. 750 ML
(25 FL OZ/3 CUPS)

1 kg (2 lb 3 oz) fresh ripe,
flavourful tomatoes
salt and freshly ground
black pepper

This is Andrea Falcone's method of making a passata to use in soups such as the Winter Tomato & Bread Soup on page 141. He includes the skins as this increases the flavour of the soup. You can also use it in place of tinned tomatoes when making a tomato sauce (see opposite).

Preheat the oven to 200°C (400°F/Gas 6). Cut the tomatoes in half (around the equator, not pole to pole) and put them cut side up in a roasting tray. Sprinkle with salt and pepper and roast for 20 minutes or until they just start to collapse and brown. Remove from the oven and put the tomatoes in a blender or food processor. Pulse to blend, until smooth. The passata will keep for up to 4 days in the fridge.

cooking dried pasta

AS A GUIDE YOU NEED 80 G
(3 OZ) PASTA FOR A STARTER
PORTION AND 100 G (3½ OZ)
FOR A MAIN COURSE

We prefer to use an Italian brand such as Barilla or De Cecco when buying dried pasta. The quality is good, the result is firm, bouncy pasta and they are very accurate with the cooking times on the packets.

Dried pasta should be cooked in the biggest pot you have. It can then move around in the water without sticking together. You don't need any oil. Make sure the water is bubbling hard when you put in the pasta.

Salt the water generously. The rule of thumb is 60 g (2 oz) salt in 6 litres (10½ pints/25 cups) water for 500 g (1 lb 2 oz) pasta. If you taste the water, it should taste like the sea, then the pasta will be tasty enough to eat on its own.

Just before you've reached the cooking time on the packet, take out a strand of pasta and test it. If it is just tender, but still has some resistance, then it is ready – 'al dente', literally 'to the tooth'.

Always transfer the al dente pasta to the warm sauce. The best way to collect the pasta is with a 'spider' (a cobweb-shaped sieve) or a pair of tongs. As you transfer the pasta a few splashes of cooking water is added to the sauce, which helps to lengthen and flavour it.

The pasta should finish cooking for a minute or two in the sauce to really absorb the flavour. Toss the pan or use tongs to move the pasta in the sauce to combine them both. Some of the starch from the pasta will release into the sauce and help thicken it. If the sauce becomes too thick, add a little of the pasta cooking water. The exception to this rule is raw sauces such as pesto, which are simply stirred through hot pasta in a bowl.

how to use... salt

In the Middle Ages salt was only used when absolutely necessary – such as for preserving – as it was very expensive, hence the traditional Tuscan bread has always been made without salt. Part of the expense resulted from a local tax on salt imposed in the 16th century across Tuscany.

Salt is an essential part of the Tuscan kitchen. Without it your food will never taste authentic. We have measured the salt quantities in some of the recipes when you cannot add salt to taste, for example to a ragù before it is cooked, to a mixture with raw eggs or to a bake. When you can, do keep tasting your food before serving it. This might sound obvious, but you would be amazed by the number of people who don't, and the end result can be disappointingly bland after all your efforts.

Adding salt can often make food taste sweeter. For example, adding the right amount of salt to a tomato sauce brings out the natural sweetness of the tomato, avoiding the need to add sugar.

Tuscan food can often be salty. To address this, if you were a little over generous with the salt, add a peeled small potato to the pot and it will absorb the salt. A squeeze of lemon juice helps, too. An average Italian pinch of salt is approximately 3 g (½ teaspoon).

chillies

Having written cookbooks for years I have now realised it is pointless to state how much fresh chilli to put into a recipe. Long red or green chillies vary so much in heat you cannot tell by looking at them. Therefore, I encourage students in our cookery classes to taste the chilli. The heat is not in the seeds but in the pith, so you need to taste the chilli from around the middle, not at either end where there may be no pith. Only by tasting it will you know how much to add to your dish.

herbs

Small pots of sage, rosemary, parsley, basil and thyme sit outside every Tuscan's house or flat where there is a little space. These provide essential flavours to Tuscan food. Only a few dried herbs will be found in the Tuscan cupboard, such as sage, oregano and fennel seeds. Parsley is easy to grow and used in abundance, and someone who is always hanging around is called *prezzemolo* (parsley) – it was Giancarlo's nickname when he was young as he was always in the kitchen.

To dry herbs at home, pick them at their peak and tie them in bunches by their stems. Hang them in a dry, airy place until completely brittle and crumbly. Put them into a bag and crush them with your hands. Pull out the stems and tip the leaves straight from the bag into jars. To dry fennel seeds, pick the yellow flower heads of wild fennel when the seeds have begun to dry on the plant. Tie, dry and store them like the herbs. The seeds and herbs will keep until the following year but will gradually lose their strength.

how to cook beans

MAKES APPROX. 1.35 KG (3 LB) COOKED BEANS

500 g (1 lb 2 oz) dried cannellini, borlotti, or other similar-sized beans
2 garlic cloves
small handful of sage leaves
3 litres (5 pints/12¾ cups) water
1–2 teaspoons salt, according to taste

Tuscans are known colloquially as *mangiafagioli* (beaneaters) and can boast over 20 varieties of bean in their region. They are said to be poor man's protein and have given valuable nutrients in the form of protein and carbohydrate to Tuscans since Etruscan times (see page 16). They form an important part of the healthy Mediterranean diet and you often find them in the diets of people who have long lives.

If you grow your own beans you know how old they are, but when we buy packets from the shops we have no idea how long they've been hanging around. The older they are the drier they are, so be prepared to cook them for as long as necessary to make sure they are soft.

Pick over the beans, discarding any stones or broken beans. Rinse the remaining beans under cold running water. To speed up the cooking time and help the beans hold their shape once cooked, soak them in plenty of cold water so that they are well covered; small beans for a minimum of 4 hours (or overnight), and large beans, such as butter beans, for at least 8 hours. To speed up the soaking process, put the washed beans into a saucepan of plenty of cold water and bring to the boil. Allow them to boil for 2 minutes then remove from the heat. Cover and let them soak for 1 hour in the warm water.

Drain the soaked beans, then put them in a heavy-based saucepan with the garlic and sage. Pour in the water, ensuring that the top of the beans are covered by a 5 cm (2 in) layer of water, and add the salt. Bring to the boil, then reduce the heat and simmer gently until tender, stirring occasionally. The cooking time will vary hugely so check the beans regularly. To give you an idea, soaked small beans take around 1 hour and large beans take around 1½ hours. Make sure they are always submerged in water, adding more as necessary. Bicarbonate of soda (baking soda) can speed up the cooking, but it affects the flavour and destroys some nutrients so we don't use it. Cool cooked beans in the cooking liquid before draining. They will keep in the fridge for up to 5 days.

For soups, or when serving with fish or meat, purée one third of the beans with a stick blender for a slightly thicker consistency, or blend all of them to a velvety cream. If serving them as they are, for a vegetable dish, dress the beans with your best peppery extra-virgin olive oil and season to taste.

Cooking beans without soaking

Beans can be cooked without any soaking; you just need to allow longer for them to cook. They are best cooked slowly in the oven. Preheat the oven to 160°C (320°F/Gas 3). Rinse the beans and pick over the beans. Put them and any flavourings into a heavy-based casserole dish and pour in enough cold water to cover them by 3 cm (1¼ in). Cover with the lid and cook in the oven for up to 2 hours or until soft.

how to make a cartouche

This is a simple trick to make a lining for a cake tin or a circle of paper to cover fruit when it's poaching. It is used a lot in Italian cooking when making cakes. It also saves washing the tin! I think it is prettier to tear the circle out so that you have rough edges which protude above the edge of the tin.

Cut or tear off a piece of baking parchment larger than the surface you are going to cover. Fold the piece of paper in half and then in half again. Now fold the edges in to make a triangle. Fold again the same way. Put the pointed end of the triangle into the centre of the tin and measure out to see where you need to cut off the excess. Either tear or cut at that point. Open out the circle and use.

how to make a cartoccio

This is a way of steaming foods but it also traps in the flavours and juices. I think it is a lovely way to cook; it's clean and simple. I used to get our boys to make their own parcels of food to cook so that they took part in cooking. They would write their names on the outside so they knew whose 'present' was whose.

To make a cartoccio, cut a rectangle of baking parchment at least 10 cm (4 in) larger than the food you are about to cook. Lay the food in the centre of the paper. Fold the long ends up to meet each other above the food. Make a fold of both pieces together of around 2 cm (¾ in) then fold again. Keep folding down until the fold is around 4 cm (1½ in) above the food. Now fold the short ends inwards to seal the parcel and trap any juices. Place the parcels on a baking tray to cook. I find this is enough to cook and hold the juices when steaming vegetables. However, if you are cooking fish *al cartoccio*, it is a good idea to wrap the paper parcel again in foil to be sure that no steam or juice leaks out.

how to store low-sugar preserves

Since we wrote our book *The Gentle Art of Preserving*, we have incorporated many of the techniques we learnt into our lives. Giancarlo's mother would have preserved vegetables and fruits throughout the season, and cured meats in winter, as she had no fridge until the 1970s. If a jam consists of over 60 per cent sugar it can be poured into sterilised jars and kept out of the fridge, as harmful bacteria cannot grow in a solution so sugary. However, we like to use little sugar in our recipes these days, so preserving under a vacuum is a better solution.

First of all, clean your jars by pouring boiling water into them up to the top (I do this in the sink) and put the lids into a bowl of just-boiled water for 10 minutes. This method is better for jars with metal lids lined with plastic coating rather than Kilner-style jars. The jars can be recycled ones but the lids should be new to ensure a tight seal.

Tip away the water from the jars using a pair of tongs. Spoon the low-sugar preserve or compote evenly between the jars and pour over the juices. The level of liquid should completely submerge the fruit, so add a little boiled water if necessary. Drain and screw on the lids with a clean cloth. The jars can either be cooled at this point and stored in the fridge for up to 2 weeks, or they can be further sterilised to extend their shelf life as follows.

Put a clean tea towel (dish towel) in the bottom of a large saucepan big enough to hold the filled and sealed jars, and deep enough to be able to cover them with water. Put the jars into the pan and put a piece of paper towel or a small cloth between all the jars. Fill the pan with water so that the jars are completely covered. Put the pan over a high heat and bring to the boil. Reduce the heat and let it bubble gently for 10 minutes, then turn off the heat. Allow the jars to cool in the pan. When the water is at room temperature, remove the jars and check that there is a depression in the lids. This means you have created a vacuum and your jars can be stored in a cool, dark place for up to 3 months. If they have not created a vacuum, store them in the fridge for up to 2 weeks.

PLUM JAM
(PAGE 63)

breakfast

breakfast

Caffè e cornetto (coffee and a croissant) is the typical morning order placed at the local bar for almost every Italian, in every Italian street, in every Italian city I have ever visited. I love this time of day; there is a busy, bustling, convivial atmosphere in a small room crowded with freshly scrubbed Italians smelling of aftershave and perfume, with freshly applied make-up, chatting, laughing, and getting their first fix of sugar and caffeine for the day ahead. But life wasn't and isn't always like this.

For our countryside-dwelling friends, who have animals to feed before themselves, breakfast is taken later. It is more substantial and perhaps more in line with my savoury tooth. In times past, *colazione* in the countryside was an array of bread, meats and cheeses always served with a jug of homemade wine. In time, the wine was replaced by a cup of milky coffee.

So, in this chapter, we have covered all the bases and included breakfasts from urban bars to rural farmhouse kitchens. We also have friends who, like many Italians, have realised they (like Giancarlo) can no longer tolerate gluten, and those who have been advised to cut sugar or carbohydrate out of their diet. Yes, diabetes and obesity are problems that face many Italians, too. For a healthier breakfast we suggest Babbo's Eggs on page 59, a slice of the *erbolata* on page 86 or a vegetable timbale from page 157.

coffee

Firstly, a little about coffee, an essential drug to every Italian I know. It was introduced to Italy through Venice from the Middle East. Initially it was thought to be an Islamic threat to the Christian world, a demon of a drink. However, after Pope Clement VIII drank a cup he proclaimed it Christian and the first coffee house or *caffè* was opened in 1683, named for the drink it sold. Fourteen billion cups of espresso are consumed each year in Italy. Each adult Italian will drink an average of four shots of coffee in a day. Coffee taken standing at the bar costs less than when it is drunk at a table as there is no clearing or service involved. Most Italians are in and out of a bar quickly, hence the lukewarm temperature of a cappuccino so you can drink and go. Ask for *caldo* if you want yours hot.

'14 billion cups of espresso are consumed each year in italy.'

Coffee-making by experienced baristas is taken seriously. As every Italian seems to be a coffee expert it is not surprising that the art of making the perfect espresso, cappuccino or macchiato time after time is treated with respect. Apparently, over 57 per cent of baristas have 10 or more years of experience and the majority are therefore of an older age. Scalded milk, a cappuccino served too hot to drink in a hurry, or an espresso without the thin layer of pale brown foam (*crema*) is not appreciated. Baristas have to observe the weather and adjust the grinding of the coffee appropriately. They have to constantly clean and brush away any used coffee grounds and maintain the machines which are their livelihood. The milk should ideally be served at 70°C (160°F) for a drink to be drunk straight away, and coffee cups should always be warm.

RISTRETTO
The most concentrated shot of coffee, taken before the water has finished dripping through the filter.

ESPRESSO OR CAFFÈ
Singolo or *doppio* (single or double) shots of the dark elixir ground to order from a mixture of Robusta and Arabica beans.

ESPRESSO LUNGO
A longer espresso, where water is allowed to drip through the filter for longer than normal.

CAPPUCCINO
The barrista's mix of a single shot of espresso in a small round cup with roughly four times the amount of milk steamed to 70°C (160°F), with foam filling the rest of the cup (the foam should be creamy and marshmallowy, with bubbles so small they're pretty much invisible).

The name comes from the 19th century *kapuziner*, a small Viennese coffee mixed with cream or milk until it resembled the colour of the Capuchin friars' habits.

Drink it before 11 am and never with or after a meal. Do dunk a biscuit into it for breakfast. Some Italians pour cereal into the cup — weird!

AMERICANO
A long black coffee.

CAFFÈ LATTE
Do say the 'caffè' with the 'latte' or you will be served a glass of warm milk. Like cappuccino, caffè latte is only permissible in the mornings.

MACCHIATO
A single espresso 'marked' with a swirl of foam.

SHAKERATO
Iced coffee served in summer, shaken over ice and usually sweetened (unless you specify *senza zucchero*), boosted with a shot of liqueur such as Frangelico if you wish.

CORRETTO
An espresso 'corrected' by alcohol, usually grappa, sambuca (Giancarlo's favourite) or brandy.

PONCE
Pronounced 'ponchay', this beverage, a sweet and powerful mixture of espresso, rum, sugar and lemon zest, is found in the Livorno area and is named after punch brought there by the British.

DECAFFEINATO
Decaffeinated coffee used to be frowned upon but is now more widely accepted.

D'ORZO
A barley coffee with a gentle taste and no caffeine, which used to be drunk in times of poverty and by the elderly, and is now popular with many young people.

MOCHA
A pleasing mixture of hot chocolate and coffee. Confusingly pronounced in the same way as the Moka pots, the little aluminum coffee makers that bubble away on stoves in every household.

breakfast in the tuscan countryside

Between our friends, breakfast in the country ranges from yoghurt with fruit, toasted Tuscan saltless bread with a tomato and green Tuscan olive oil, or, for Giancarlo's father, it was bread with a ripe jammy fig or a wedge of fresh melon. Antonella Secciani prepares a spread of salami, finnochiona, cheese, fresh broad beans, raw artichokes in pinzimonio (an oil dressing), leftover *pappa al pomodoro* and a jug of homemade red wine for the owners and staff at the *agriturismo* (farm B&B). It is eaten between 9 and 10 am after sorting out the animals on the farm and taking the kids to school.

toasted bread with tomatoes & olive oil

**SERVES 1 PERSON
(NOT FOR SHARING)**

1 garlic clove, peeled
2 thick slices crusty bread,
    toasted
1 ripe tomato
good-quality olive oil,
    for drizzling
salt, to taste

Alma and Vincenzo Longhitano run the busy Trattoria il Corso in the unpronounceable Roccatederighi, a hilltop town in the Maremma area of southern Tuscany. We went to learn some local specialities, but having got up early to make our way through the winding roads I became rather more captivated by her breakfast than the pasta. Alma made herself *pane pomodoro,* **a simple little number of crusty bread rubbed with a tomato, then smothered in their local olive oil. She added a little salt and ate the lot despite me commenting on how luscious it looked and taking photographs; sadly she wasn't going to be budged from her brekkie.**

Lightly rub the garlic clove over one side of each piece of toast. Cut the tomato in half and rub it over the toast, on the same sides you rubbed the garlic. It will naturally tear and break down, soaking into the bread. Drizzle over some of your best olive oil and scatter the toast with salt. Eat all by yourself and make sure the oil and tomato dribbles down your chin in proper Tuscan fashion.

babbo's eggs

**SERVES
2 PEOPLE**

300 g (10½ oz) Homemade
    Tomato Sauce (see page 40)
4 eggs
salt and freshly ground
    black pepper
small handful of parsley,
    finely chopped (optional)
toasted bread, to serve
    (optional)

This is one of our favourite breakfasts in the Caldesi household. We all like to eat it and it is easy to rustle up before the kids head out to school. It has a long history: Giancarlo's father used to concoct it for himself after an early morning start in the fields as a mid-morning breakfast. In the Tuscan dialect 'daddy' is *babbo,* **hence the name. We always have a plastic box of tomato sauce in the fridge so it is quick to put together.**

Pour the sauce into a large frying pan and warm over a medium heat. Crack the eggs into the sauce in 4 places, keeping them separate from one another if your pan is large enough. Season the eggs with salt and pepper and cover the pan with a lid. Continue to cook for around 5 minutes or until the eggs are done to your liking. Serve on its own, scattered with parsley, or with toasted bread.

TOASTED
BREAD WITH
TOMATOES
& OLIVE OIL
(PAGE 59)

PICKLED
VEGETABLES
(PAGE 78)

plum jam

MAKES APPROX. 2 KG
(4 LB 6 OZ)

3 kg (6 lb 6 oz) ripe plums,
    washed, cut in half
    and stoned
900 g (2 lb/scant 4 cups)
    caster (superfine) sugar

This perfectly simple recipe is from Graziella, the chef from La Mandriola, a stunning *agriturismo* on top of a hill near Volterra. We stayed here and Graziella showed us how she made her soft-set plum jam, which is rather like a compote. It is ideal for pouring over soft ricotta and topping with chopped walnuts for breakfast. Alternatively, stir it into yoghurt or enjoy it on toast. We often make half this amount and keep it in the fridge for up to a month. It doesn't have a high sugar content so cannot be guaranteed to last out of the fridge, unless the jars are sterilised. If you make this large batch and wish to keep it for longer, follow the instructions for preserving a low-sugar recipe in jars on page 50.

Put the plums in a large heavy-based saucepan with the sugar and bring to the boil over a gentle heat. Let the jam bubble away, stirring frequently, until the fruit is soft. This will take between 30 minutes and 1 hour, depending on the ripeness of the fruit. Remove from the heat.

The jam can now be puréed with a stick blender for a smooth finish or left with the softened plums still intact for a little texture. Pour into clean jars while hot and screw on clean lids. Allow to cool and store in the fridge for up to 1 month.

fig & mascarpone or ricotta crostini with honey

**SERVES
2 PEOPLE**

2 thick slices country-
 style bread
125 g (4 oz/½ cup) ricotta
 or mascarpone
2 ripe figs or other soft fruit,
 washed and trimmed
50 g (2 oz/½ cup) shelled
 walnuts, roughly chopped
mild runny honey, such
 as acacia, for drizzling

We have a lovely old photograph of Giancarlo's father, Memmo, picking figs with our son Giorgio when he was little. Giorgio is carrying a little basket and looking up at his grandfather with joy as he fills it with ripe figs from the tree outside Memmo's house.

 Do use the ripest figs when in season, when they are naturally sweet and jammy. Alternatively, use berries, peach or nectarine slices, or persimmon. Even without the bread, this is a wonderful concoction. Most hotels in Italy will offer fresh ricotta, fruit and honey, and some have nuts on offer, so I often rustle this up for a healthy breakfast when staying away from home.

Toast the bread on both sides. Spread the cheese thickly on one side of each slice. Now slice or squash the figs, if really ripe and jammy, on top, scatter over the walnuts and drizzle with a little honey.

coffee & ricotta shots

**SERVES
4–6 PEOPLE,
IN SMALL LIQUEUR GLASSES**

250 g (9 oz/1 cup) ricotta,
    drained
4 tablespoons cold espresso
3 teaspoons caster (superfine)
    sugar, plus more, to taste
2 teaspoons Cognac
20 g (¾ oz) dark (bittersweet)
    chocolate (minimum 70%
    cocoa solids)

**This is one of my favourite recipes in the book. It is an old way of
eating ricotta in Tuscany as a breakfast or *merenda* (an afternoon
snack). It is simple and effective as well as light to eat and not too
sweet. I like to serve this in shot glasses for breakfast or after dinner.**

Whisk the ricotta in a bowl with the coffee, sugar and the Cognac. Taste and
adjust the sweetness as necessary, adding more sugar if you wish. Spoon into
glasses, taking care not to splash it onto the sides of the glass. Use a sharp
knife to shave curls of chocolate and scatter them over the top. Keep them
in the fridge for up to 1 day until you are ready to eat them. Serve chilled.

blackberry compote

MAKES APPROX. 450 G (1 LB)

500 g (1 lb 2 oz) blackberries
1–2 tablespoons cherry brandy
 (optional)
1–2 tablespoons caster
 (superfine) sugar
1 teaspoon lemon juice

Preserving fruit is something many countryside-dwelling Tuscans do. Most of our Italian friends never weigh anything or follow an exact recipe, as the proportions of fruit and sugar depend on the size and sweetness of the fruit in season. Our friend Nick Sandler, a keen preserver whom we met through writing our book *The Gentle Art of Preserving*, has followed in the Italian tradition of storing summer fruits for winter use and gave us a jar of his compote after a blackberry picking session. A *composta* such as this is ideal at breakfast with yoghurt and walnuts, or with cream for a dessert. Our son Flavio puts a spoonful on his oats and yoghurt and it is superb.

Depending on the sweetness of the blackberries you can use more or less sugar. We try to use the minimum. The cherry brandy is optional; leave it out or substitute it with brandy or rum. As this recipe makes a small amount you can simply keep the compote in the fridge without worrying about preserving techniques, but I have given the instructions for sterilising should you want to make more. The filled jars do need to be boiled to create a vacuum as there is not enough sugar or alcohol alone to preserve them out of the fridge.

Put the blackberries in a saucepan with the other ingredients and bring to a gentle boil. Heat through for 5 minutes, stirring gently. The berries will start to release water and soften. Small blackberries will take just 5 minutes to soften, but large ones can take up to 10 minutes.

Taste the liquid and adjust the brandy (if using) and sugar as necessary. The compote can be eaten straight away (it is delicious warm with vanilla ice cream) or left to cool. It will keep in the fridge for up to 3 days. Alternatively, follow the instructions on page 50 for preserving the blackberries in jars (we use 2 × 225 g/8 oz jars).

breakfast in the tuscan city

CIOCCOLATO CALDO

hot chocolate

**MAKES 400 ML
(13 FL OZ/1¾ CUPS),
ENOUGH FOR 8 ESPRESSO CUPS**

100 g (3½ oz) dark (bittersweet)
  chocolate (minimum 70%
  cocoa solids), broken
  into squares
200 ml (7 fl oz/scant 1 cup)
  double (heavy) cream
100 ml (3½ fl oz/scant ½ cup)
  whole (full-fat) milk
1 tablespoon salted butter

This decadent, intense hot chocolate has been served in Florence's best cafes for centuries. The bittersweet flavour comes from using really good-quality chocolate. Vestri in Borgo degli Albizi is a small shop stuffed with chocolate treats including huge slabs of pistachio or gianduja chocolates as well as an urn constantly warming dense hot chocolate that is slowly trickled into a small cup. This is our version, which is rich so we serve it in warm espresso cups (see picture on page 70). It can be topped with a dollop of whipped cream.

Warm the ingredients slowly together in a small saucepan, stirring constantly, until smooth and glossy. Drink straight away.

sienese almond biscuits

MAKES
APPROX. 36 BISCUITS

400 g (14 oz/4 cups) ground
    almonds (almond meal)
2 teaspoons almond extract
175 g (6 oz/1½ cups)
    icing (confectioners') sugar
    for the biscuits, plus 100 g
    (3½ oz/generous ¾ cup)
    for dusting
1 teaspoon baking powder
175–200 g (6–7 oz) egg whites
    (about 4 large egg whites)

**A freshly baked batch of these biscuits (see opposite, centre)
makes the house smell warm and inviting.**

Preheat the oven to 160°C (320°F/Gas 3) and line a baking sheet with
baking parchment. Combine the ground almonds, almond extract, 175 g
(6 oz/1½ cups) icing sugar and the baking powder in a large mixing bowl.
Beat the egg whites in a separate clean bowl with a whisk until they form
a soft foam, then add them to the almond mixture a little at a time. Stir with
a large wooden spoon to form a thick paste – the mixture should be sticky
but not runny. You may have a little egg white left, which you can discard.
Put the extra icing sugar for dusting in a separate bowl.

Use 2 dessertspoons to form about 36 quenelles (raised oval shapes)
by transferring the mixture between the spoons, then drop them gently
into the bowl of icing sugar to coat them.

Remove each quenelle gently with a slotted spoon and place them on
the lined baking sheet, spaced apart. Bake the biscuits for 20–25 minutes
or until lightly golden. Remove from the oven and leave to cool on a wire rack
before serving. They can be stored for up to 1 week in an airtight container.

aniseed biscuits

MAKES
APPROX. 24 BISCUITS

150 g (5 oz/⅔ cup) caster
    (superfine) sugar
150 ml (5 fl oz/⅔ cup) water
75 g (2½ oz) runny honey
250 g (9 oz/2 cups) '00'
    or gluten-free flour,
    plus extra for dusting
1 heaped teaspoon bicarbonate
    of soda (baking soda)
50 g (2 oz) candied fruit,
    finely diced
75 g (2½ oz) walnuts,
    finely chopped
finely grated zest of 1 orange
1 heaped teaspoon aniseed
    or ground star anise
10 g (¼ oz) mixture of ground
    coriander, cinnamon,
    cloves, nutmeg (to taste)

**These biscuits are deliciously delicate (see opposite, top right). Vary
the spices as you wish – the darker the spices, the darker the biscuit.**

Preheat the oven to 160°C (300°F/Gas 2) and line 2 baking trays with baking
parchment. Put the sugar, water and honey in a saucepan over a high heat
until it reaches a gentle boil and the sugar has dissolved.

Put the rest of the ingredients in a mixing bowl and pour the hot sugar
syrup into it, taking care not to splash yourself. Stir until it forms a dough.
Tip the dough out onto a floured work surface, divide it in half and make
2 long sausages measuring approximately 3 cm (1¼ in) wide. Cut each
sausage into 12 equal-sized pieces. Roll each piece into a ball the size of
a walnut and coat it in flour. Place the balls onto the lined baking trays,
spaced about 5 cm (2 in) apart. Bake for 10 minutes or until the tops crack
and they become golden brown. Remove from the oven and allow to cool
on a wire rack. Eat straight away or store in airtight container for up to 3 days.

florentine cake

SERVES
6 PEOPLE

FOR THE SPONGE
2 large eggs
200 g (7 oz/1 scant cup) caster
     (superfine) sugar
6 tablespoons extra-virgin
     olive oil
finely grated zest of 1 medium
     orange
150 ml (5 fl oz/⅔ cup)
     whole (full-fat) milk
250 g (9 oz/2 cups) '00'
     or plain (all-purpose) flour
2 teaspoons baking powder
pinch of salt

FOR THE FILLING
350 ml (12 fl oz/1½ cups)
     whipping cream
25 g (1 oz) icing
     (confectioners') sugar,
     plus extra for dusting
cocoa powder, for dusting
     (optional)

GLUTEN-FREE SPONGE

4 large eggs
225 g (8 oz) unsalted butter
     at room temperature
225 g (8 oz/scant 2 cups)
     cornflour (cornstarch)
225 g (8 oz/1 cup) caster
     (superfine) sugar
2 teaspoons baking powder
1 teaspoon vanilla extract
pinch of salt
finely grated zest of
     1 orange (optional)

These dramatic orange-scented cakes dominate the pastry shops of Florence at the time of Carnevale towards the end of January and through February. They are usually made in a large square or rectangular tin and decorated with the *giglio* fleur-de-lys symbol of Florence. They are often served plain for breakfast but I prefer mine stuffed full of sweetened whipped cream.

Preheat the oven to 180°C (350°F/Gas 4). Generously butter a rectangular loose-bottomed cake tin measuring around 35 × 12 × 3 cm (14 × 5 × 1¼ in), or a square or round 20–24 cm (8–9 in) springform cake tin. The sponge will be cut horizontally through the middle, making two halves.

To make the sponge, whisk the eggs and sugar together in a bowl or a stand mixer for around 5 minutes until pale and fluffy. Pour in the oil, orange zest and milk and whisk again briefly until blended. Sift in the flour and baking powder, add the salt, and whisk once more. Pour the batter into the prepared tin and bake for 20–25 minutes or until the sponge feels firm to the touch and a skewer inserted into the middle of the cake comes out clean. Remove from the oven and leave for 10 minutes to cool in the tin. Run a knife between the cake and the tin to loosen it, then unclip the tin or push it up by the base and put the cake on a wire rack to cool.

Meanwhile, make the filling by whipping the cream and icing sugar together in a bowl until it forms soft peaks. Split the cake in half by cutting through the middle horizontally with a large serrated knife. Spread the bottom half with a thick layer of cream, then top with the other half. Run a clean finger or palette knife along the sides of the cake to smooth away any cream spilling out and neaten the edges. Dust with sifted icing sugar and serve as it is or make a stencil and scatter over cocoa powder. Put the cake into the fridge to set firm for 1 hour and serve chilled. It will keep for up to 3 days in the fridge and in my opinion seems to improve with time. For a gluten-free sponge, follow the recipe below.

●

Variation: Gluten-free sponge
Put all the ingredients in a bowl and beat with an electric whisk until smooth. Pour into the prepared tin and cook as above.

●

choux buns

When Catherine de' Medici left Florence in 1533 to marry the Duke of Orleans in France she took her entire court with her, including her chefs. Her head chef Pantarelli is said to have invented the first choux-style pastry. Later, in the 19th century, the French chef Marie-Antoine Carême tweaked the recipe and made small buns from it that looked like little cabbages, hence the use of the French name 'choux'.

Known as *bignè* (pronounced 'bin-gneh') in Italy, these tiny little delights are hard to resist at breakfast time with a cappuccino or caffè.

**MAKES APPROX.
40 CHOUX BUNS**

FOR THE CHOUX PASTRY
100 g (3½ oz) salted butter
240 ml (8½ fl oz/1 cup) water
1 teaspoon caster (superfine) sugar
150 g (5 oz/generous 1 cup) strong white flour
4 eggs, beaten

FOR THE PASTRY CREAM
500 ml (17 fl oz/2¼ cups) whole (full-fat) milk
seeds scraped from 1 vanilla pod (bean) or 1 teaspoon vanilla extract
3 egg yolks
75 g (2½ oz/⅓ cup) caster (superfine) sugar
45 g (1½ oz/⅓ cup) cornflour (cornstarch)
75 g (2½ oz) dark (bittersweet) chocolate (minimum 70% cocoa solids), grated

TO SERVE
icing (confectioners') sugar, for dusting
200 g (7 oz) white, milk or dark (bittersweet) chocolate (or a mix of chocolates), chopped (optional)

Preheat the over to 200°C (400°F/Gas 6). Line 1–2 baking trays with baking parchment. To make the choux pastry, put the butter in a medium saucepan with the water and sugar over a medium heat. As soon as the butter has melted and the mixture has come to the boil, tip in the flour in one go and beat with a wooden spoon until the flour is well incorporated. Remove the pan from the heat. Now, using a handheld or electric whisk, add the eggs a little at a time until you have a smooth, glossy dough.

Put the dough into a piping bag fitted with a plain round 1 cm (½ in) nozzle. Pipe out around 40 little mounds of the mixture approximately 3 cm (1¼ in) wide and 2 cm (¾ in) high onto the prepared trays. They should be spaced apart by around 5 cm (2 in) as they will puff up during cooking. Bake the choux buns for 10 minutes, then turn the oven down to 170°C (340°F/Gas 3) and bake for a further 10–15 minutes, or until golden brown and firm inside. Remove from the oven and leave to cool on a wire rack.

To make the pastry cream, heat the milk with the vanilla in a medium saucepan over a medium heat. While it's warming up, whisk together the egg yolks, sugar and cornflour in a bowl. Whisk a ladleful of the warmed milk into the bowl, then pour this mixture into the saucepan with the rest of the milk. Stir with a wooden spoon until the cream thickens – it will only take a few minutes – then remove from the heat. Divide the cream between 2 heatproof bowls and add the grated chocolate to one bowl. Stir through until melted. Cover the surface of the pastry cream in both bowls with cling film (plastic wrap) to avoid a skin forming, then set aside and allow to cool.

Put one of the creams into a piping bag fitted with a 5 mm (¼ in) nozzle and pipe it into half of the choux buns. To do this, force the piping bag nozzle into the bun and squeeze to fill. Do the same with the other bowl of cream and the remaining buns. Lay the buns on a rack and either dust them with icing sugar before transferring them to a serving platter, or cover the tops with chocolate as follows: melt the chocolate in the microwave or in a heatproof bowl over a pan of simmering water, making sure the bowl doesn't touch the water. Spoon the melted chocolate over the buns.

For **gluten-free choux pastry** follow the recipe above but use 3 medium eggs and gluten-free flour in place of the strong flour. You may find they are a little flatter than the wheat flour choux, but they taste just as good.

puff pastry pie with cheese & ham

**SERVES
8–10 PEOPLE**

2 × 320 g (11½ oz) sheets
all-butter puff pastry
(35 × 23 cm/14 × 9 in)
125 g (4 oz) Homemade Tomato
Sauce (see page 40)
or Fresh Tomato Passata
(see page 41)
salt and freshly ground black
pepper (if using passata)
150 g (5 oz) fontina, asiago,
Gruyère or Cheddar, finely
grated
150 g (5 oz) cooked smoked
or unsmoked ham, thinly
sliced
1 egg, beaten with a pinch
of salt and sugar

**I always look out for savoury options for breakfast in Italian bars.
If I am lucky there will be these warm tomato, ham and cheese pastry
slices on offer. They are named after the famous northern combination
of chicken escalopes with cheese and ham. Do get good ham with
plenty of flavour. Whether it is smoked or unsmoked it is up to you,
but the paper-thin slices filled with water offer nothing to the recipe.**

Preheat the oven to 200°C (400°F/Gas 6). Unwrap the pastry and stretch the
first piece out onto a baking tray lined with baking parchment. Spread it with
the tomato sauce, leaving a border of 2 cm (¾ in) clear around the edges.
If you are using passata, it is generally unseasoned so sprinkle with a little salt
and pepper as necessary. Now scatter over the cheese, followed by the ham,
respecting the clear border.

Lay the second sheet of pastry on a lightly floured surface and score
shallow, diagonal cuts across its surface, to make a diamond pattern. Lay the
scored pastry over the first sheet. Use your fingertips to push the two layers
of pastry together around the edges and seal with the prongs of a fork to make
little lines around the border. Brush the top with a thin layer of the seasoned
beaten egg (this will make it more golden). Keep the rest of the egg for later.
Use the tip of a sharp knife to make around 10 small holes in the pastry, to
allow the air to escape.

Let the pie rest in the fridge or a cool place for 10 minutes, then brush it with
egg again. Bake for 20 minutes or until golden brown, then turn the oven down
to 170°C (340°F/Gas 3) and bake for a further 10–15 minutes. Remove from
the oven and allow to cool for a few minutes before serving. It is also good
eaten at room temperature.

pickled vegetables

SERVES
12–14 PEOPLE

1 kg (2 lb 3 oz) vegetables,
    such as (bell) peppers,
    carrots, cucumber,
    cauliflower, green beans,
    celery, radish
50 g (2 oz) fine salt

FOR THE PICKLING LIQUID
25 g (1 oz/scant 2 tablespoons)
    caster (superfine) sugar
500 ml (17 fl oz/2¼ cups)
    hot water
10 black peppercorns
1 teaspoon coriander seeds
½ teaspoon dried chilli flakes
500 ml (17 fl oz/2¼ cups)
    white wine vinegar
1 bay leaf
2 fat garlic cloves, peeled
    and finely sliced

This makes a fairly small batch of pickles that can be kept in the fridge. There is no need to sterilise the bottles or make the vegetables too salty or vinegary in order to preserve them. I prefer not to cook them as I like the crunch in this method of pickling. They never last long in our house as we love to eat them with cheeses or salami, cured meats or on mixed plates of antipasti.

Cut the vegetables into bite-sized pieces of similar scale. I like to cut the carrots into batons to avoid the school canteen look, the cauliflower into small florets and the peppers into strips. Cucumbers are best deseeded and green beans cut into manageable lengths. Toss them in a large plastic or glass bowl with the salt, then put a side plate on top of the vegetables, inside the bowl. Weigh the plate down with a milk carton or some jars and store in the fridge for 8 hours.

Meanwhile, make the pickling liquid. Put the sugar in a small saucepan with the water and spices. Heat for 5 minutes, stirring with a wooden spoon until the sugar has dissolved and its crystals can't be felt as you stir. Pour the sugary water into a large plastic or glass bowl and add the vinegar, bay leaf and garlic. Stir through, cover and allow to cool.

Remove the vegetables from the fridge and wash them in cold water. Taste them and if they are still very salty leave them to soak in a bowl of cold water for around 30 minutes. Taste again and, when they are just right, drain away the water. Tip the vegetables into the bowl with the vinegary mixture, stir through and cover. Transfer to the fridge to chill overnight.

The pickles are now ready to eat or can be stored in very clean jars in the fridge for up to a month. Make sure the vegetables are always covered with the liquid or they will begin to dry out.

lunch

lunch

Italians still take their *l'ora di pranzo* (lunch hour) as a sacred time to eat good food, catch up with family or friends and relax, many still finding time to take a short nap. According to statistics agency ISTAT, over 74 per cent of Italians still manage to eat lunch at home.

Unemployment and the economic downturn during the country's longest post-war recession means money is tight and it goes further on food prepared at home than eaten out. Many young adults cannot afford to move out and it's not unusual to find children still living at home until the age of 30. Older relatives are looked after by the family as much as possible and often a retired mum at home will look after her grandchildren so that their parents can work, so lunch at home could easily be a three or four generational affair.

Those in cities go to local, independent trattorie that serve good and inexpensive food cooked on the premises, and offer perhaps a two-course lunch from a limited menu. Or, they go out for a freshly-made *panino*. Italy has still not surrendered to our sandwich-at-the-desk culture and most Italians care very much about what they eat.

I was horrified to be told that in a school near us in the UK teachers and students were given their lunch in a polystyrene box so that they can eat in a 15-minute break while they go from classroom to classroom. Any of our Italian friends would be aghast by this lack of respect for food and for the time given to it.

We try to follow the Italian system wherever we are. *L'ora di pranzo* is a break from work and time to enjoy food prepared quickly at home or in a local trattoria. This chapter is full of quick and easy meals that take less than 40 minutes to make, from start to finish. Most Italians will eat a bowl of pasta at home with a ragù or homemade sauce. The ragù recipes are in the fresh pasta section on page 161 but they also go well with dried pasta so do make a batch on a weekend and use it up during the week, Italian style.

When Giancarlo was growing up his father would collect fresh herbs and vegetables every day from the fields and his tiny herb garden. These would form lunch or be served with a bigger meal later that day. This meant that Giancarlo's family were always eating seasonally. In winter, leaves of cavolo nero were picked after the first frost and made into Black Kale Bruschetta (see page 86). In summer, salads were made such as panzanella, a simple dish of tomato, cucumber and yesterday's bread soaked in water.

courgette & tomato ragù

**SERVES
6 PEOPLE**

6 tablespoons extra-virgin
olive oil

1 onion, peeled and roughly
chopped

2 garlic cloves, peeled
and lightly crushed

350 g (12 oz) courgettes
(zucchini), sliced into rounds
(a mixture of green and
yellow, if possible)

salt and freshly ground
black pepper

200 g (7 oz) ripe, flavourful
tomatoes (round, cherry
or plum), cut into 1 cm
(½ in) cubes

125 g (4 oz) mozzarella,
roughly torn

15 g (½ oz) parsley, roughly
chopped

15 g (½ oz) basil leaves,
roughly torn

This delicately flavoured dish is a little like a French ratatouille. It is best made with summer produce to really appreciate the flavours. I like to eat it in a bowl for a quick lunch or serve it as a side dish for grilled meats. If you leave out the cheese it is lovely with grilled fish, too. Alternatively, add a poached egg and call it breakfast, or stir in some hot pasta shells and it will be a perfect pasta sauce. It keeps well for a couple of days in the fridge and is easily warmed through on the hob or in the microwave, making it a perfect lunchtime meal.

Heat the oil in a large non-stick frying pan over a medium heat. Add the onion and garlic and fry for about 10 minutes until the onion is translucent. Add the diced courgettes to the pan, season with salt and pepper, and toss through. Cook the courgettes for a few minutes, stirring frequently, until they start to become golden. Stir in the tomatoes and cook for a couple of minutes until they have just begun to soften and the courgettes are al dente. Serve straight away while the courgettes and tomatoes are still steaming hot, topped with the mozzarella and herbs.

a herbed dish

SERVES
8 PEOPLE

10 eggs
175 g (6 oz) leaves such as
    watercress, parsley, basil
    and spinach, roughly
    chopped
100 g (3½ oz) grated Parmesan
1 level teaspoon fine salt
freshly ground black pepper,
    to taste
½ teaspoon grated nutmeg
3 tablespoons extra-virgin
    olive oil

'From all flowers and other herbs aforementioned, whatever kind you like, you can make a herbed dish (*erbolato*) with cheese and eggs and spices, and it should be cooked in the oven or between baking pans.' This passage is from the medieval cookbook by the Anonimo Toscano, an anonymous Tuscan chef who wrote down his collection of recipes in the 1300s. An *erbolato* is a sort of medieval frittata made from seasonal herbs. His recipe works just as well for a brunch or lunch today.

Preheat the oven to 170°C (340°F/Gas 3) and line a flan dish (approximately 22 cm/9 in in diameter and 2.5 cm/1 in deep) with baking parchment.

Whisk the eggs in a bowl until blended, then stir in the rest of the ingredients, except the oil.

Pour the oil onto the parchment and wipe or brush it to coat, then pour in the frittata mixture. Bake for 30 minutes. Remove from the oven and serve hot or at room temperature, on its own or with a simple cucumber and tomato salad (see page 218). When cool it will keep in the fridge for 2 days. Simply reheat a slice or two in the microwave when you feel peckish!

black kale bruschetta

SERVES
6 PEOPLE

FOR THE SAUTÉED BLACK KALE
1 head cavolo nero leaves,
    washed and roughly chopped
6 tablespoons extra-virgin
    olive oil
2 garlic cloves, peeled and
    roughly chopped
fresh red chilli, to taste,
    roughly chopped
salt and freshly ground
    black pepper

TO SERVE
1 × 400 g (14 oz) tin
    cannellini beans (optional)
6 thick slices of crusty bread
1 garlic clove, peeled
½ lemon, for squeezing

Daniela Fiaschi, the chef from Agriturismo La Mandriola in Lajatico, showed me how to eat sautéed black kale (cavolo nero), the winter cabbage that originates from Tuscany, in her favourite way.

Bring a pan of salted water to the boil and add the cavolo nero. Cook the cavolo nero for 5–10 minutes until soft, then drain, reserving a little of the cooking water, and set aside.

Heat 3 tablespoons of the oil in a frying pan over a medium heat. Add the chopped garlic, chilli, and a pinch of salt and pepper, and fry for 2 minutes, taking care not to let the garlic brown. Add the cavolo nero, and toss well to combine. Cook for a few minutes, adding a little of the cooking water if necessary so that the cavolo nero doesn't burn. When the leaves are soft and tender (try one) it is ready. If using the beans, warm them in a small pan in the liquid from the tin, then drain in a sieve.

Toast the bread on both sides, rub with peeled garlic and pour over a little of the remaining olive oil. Top with the cavolo nero, the beans (if using), a squeeze of lemon juice, to taste, and the remaining olive oil.

sardine, borlotti & celery salad

**SERVES
6 PEOPLE**

¼ red onion, peeled and
    thinly sliced into half-moons
10 cherry tomatoes, halved
2 celery stalks, finely cut
    on the diagonal
1 small yellow (bell) pepper,
    halved, cored and seeds
    removed, and cut into
    thin strips
240 g (9 oz) cooked and drained
    borlotti or cannellini beans,
    or use tinned
1 tablespoon fresh oregano
    leaves or ½ teaspoon
    dried oregano
fresh red chilli, finely chopped,
    to taste, or ¼ teaspoon
    dried chilli flakes
2 tablespoons red wine vinegar
5 tablespoons extra-virgin
    olive oil
salt and freshly ground
    black pepper
2 × 120 g (4 oz) tins sardines
    in olive oil, drained (170 g/
    6 oz net weight)
small handful of basil leaves
    and yellow young celery
    leaves, to garnish

A simple combination of cooked cannellini beans, tinned tuna and onions is commonplace on the Tuscan table. We like to use tinned sardines as they are sustainable, economical and just as nutritious as their fresh counterparts. Whichever bean you use – borlotti beans, cannellini or similar beans – they are all equally good. To cook them from scratch, see page 44. To make the salad more substantial, add a handful of boiled and peeled quail's eggs.

When Giancarlo was growing up he rarely saw a fresh fish as he lived too far from the sea. Therefore, salted fish such as herrings or sardines, or jars of tuna in oil sold at the local market were a treat. He often tells our children that one supper time, as the youngest in the family, he was simply given the 'smell' of a canned and salted herring. His father wiped the fish onto a piece of bread and Giancarlo had to be happy with that while the adult members of the family shared the fish.

Put the sliced onions in a bowl of cold water and leave to soak for around 10–15 minutes. (This will make them less potent.) Drain well.

Put the tomatoes, celery, pepper, beans, oregano and chilli in a large bowl, add the soaked and drained onions, and mix with a large spoon. Splash over the vinegar and 4 tablespoons of the oil, season with salt and pepper and stir again. Break the sardines into the salad. Gently stir to combine, without flaking the fish. Taste and add more seasoning or chilli as necessary. (At this point, before adding the herbs, the salad will keep well in the fridge for a couple of days in a container.)

To serve, arrange the salad on a large plate. Tear over the basil and celery leaves, and drizzle over the remaining olive oil.

A HERBED
DISH
(PAGE 86)

TUSCAN
SPRING SALAD
(PAGE 90)

SARDINE,
BORLOTTI &
CELERY SALAD
(PAGE 87)

FARRO,
COURGETTE,
MINT & WALNUT
SALAD
(PAGE 91)

tuscan spring salad

SERVES
4–6 PEOPLE

200 g (7 oz) celeriac, cleaned
150 g (5 oz) white cabbage
1 green apple
1 celery stalk, finely sliced on
    the diagonal, and a handful
    of celery leaves, torn
150 g (5 oz) Pecorino or
    Manchego, shaved
75 g (2½ oz) flaked (slivered)
    almonds, toasted and
    roughly chopped

FOR THE DRESSING
4 tablespoons extra-virgin
    olive oil
juice of 1 small lemon
2 teaspoons runny mild honey
salt and freshly ground
    black pepper

This is such a refreshing, pretty salad to make. I crave foods such as this in early spring as a contrast to heavier foods. I use an old cheese grater to shave the vegetables but you could use a vegetable peeler, mandoline or the slicing blade of a food processor. I saw this salad at Montisi olive oil festival where they dressed finely sliced cabbage with the new season's olive oil. Celeriac is not used so much in Tuscany (it is more of a northern Italian vegetable), however it works brilliantly here, as would raw shaved swede. Pears can be used to substitute apples, green grapes give a jewelled effect and I like to add a few petals from the first primroses of the year.

First, make the dressing, as you will need it to dress the apple as soon as the apple is sliced, to stop the slices going brown. Whisk the ingredients together in a bowl with a generous pinch of salt and pepper. Taste and adjust the sweetness and saltiness to your liking.

To make the salad, shave the celeriac, cabbage and apple (leave the skin on the apple) and immediately toss them in a bowl with the dressing. Add the torn celery leaves and cut stalks, and assemble the salad on a large board or serving plate.

Scatter the cheese and almonds over the salad, and grind over a few twists of black pepper. Serve straight away or leave in the fridge until you are ready to serve. Most salads are ruined after a night in the fridge but this will actually keep well for a day or two, even if it loses its initial beauty.

farro, courgette, mint & walnut salad

**SERVES
6 PEOPLE**

2 courgettes (zucchini), cut
　　on the diagonal into
　　5 mm- (¼ in-) thick slices
6 tablespoons extra-virgin
　　olive oil
salt and freshly ground
　　black pepper
small handful of spring onions
　　(scallions), cut in half
　　horizontally and lengthways
　　into strips
150 g (5 oz) farro, brown rice
　　or oat groats
1 sprig of rosemary, leaves
　　picked
1 garlic clove, peeled
fresh red chilli, finely chopped,
　　to taste, or ¼ teaspoon dried
　　chilli flakes
2 tablespoons balsamic vinegar
1 ripe avocado, stoned, peeled
　　and sliced

TO SERVE
1 tablespoon good-quality
　　extra-virgin olive oil
large handful of roughly
　　torn mint leaves
25 g (1 oz) walnuts, roughly
　　chopped

It is said that the Roman soldiers were victorious as, quite simply, their diets were better than their competitors'. Centurions were given farro, an ancient grain, to carry with them on journeys by foot. This was boiled up into a thick porridge (oatmeal) – sometimes in their metal helmets – over a fire. The slowly released carbohydrate kept them well-nourished and enabled them to fight for longer than the other soldiers.

Farro, also known as (but slightly different to) spelt, einkorn or emmer, is available in health food shops and some supermarkets. It has a nutty taste and chewy texture – we love it. It is used in the north of Tuscany to make soups, salads and even cakes. The pre-cooked version, *dicocco*, takes only 10 minutes to cook whereas the uncooked whole grain can take up to 25 minutes, so make sure you know which one you have. It is low in gluten but if you want to make the salad gluten-free, substitute farro for brown rice or gluten-free oat groats.

Preheat the oven to 200°C (400°F/Gas 6) and line a baking tray with baking parchment. Put the sliced courgettes in a bowl with 2 tablespoons of the olive oil, and a generous pinch of salt and pepper. Toss to combine, then lay them on the lined tray (keep the bowl for the onions). Roast for 10 minutes (there is no need to turn them over), then remove from the oven. Toss the spring onions in the bowl in the residual oil, and scatter them over the courgettes (keep the bowl again for the dressing). Roast for another 7–10 minutes, until both vegetables are lightly browned, then remove from the oven and set aside.

While the vegetables are roasting, bring a pan of generously salted water to the boil. Wash the uncooked farro grains in a sieve under cold running water and drop them into the pan of boiling water. Cook for 10 minutes if using pre-cooked farro, or 25–30 minutes if using the uncooked grain. It should swell during cooking but still have bite to each grain, so keep trying it when you are near the end of the cooking time until you are happy with the texture.

While the farro cooks, make a *battuto* with the rosemary, garlic, a good pinch of salt and pepper, and chilli (see page 29). Mix the *battuto* in the bowl with the remaining oil and the balsamic vinegar to make the dressing. When the farro is cooked, drain it well and mix it with the dressing in the bowl.

Arrange the dressed farro on a large wooden board or on a serving platter. Lay the slices of avocado over the farro, followed by the roasted courgettes and spring onions. Drizzle over 1 tablespoon of good olive oil and finish by scattering over the mint leaves and walnuts. Serve straight away or leave to cool to room temperature.

tiziana's stuffed aubergines

SERVES
6 PEOPLE

3–4 tablespoons extra-virgin
    olive oil
2 aubergines (eggplant),
    sliced into 1 cm- (½ in-)
    thick lengths
salt and freshly ground
    black pepper
250 g (9 oz/1 cup) ricotta,
    drained
small handful of chives,
    finely chopped (optional)
small handful of mint leaves,
    finely chopped
10 g (½ oz) grated Parmesan
6 tablespoons Homemade
    Tomato Sauce (see page 40)
    or Fresh Tomato Passata
    (see page 41)

This is Giancarlo's cousin Tiziana's recipe from Buonconvento in Tuscany. She makes stuffed aubergines (eggplant) quickly for a standby lunch or starter. They keep well in the fridge so you can prepare them the day before and cook them just before serving.

Preheat the oven to 180°C (350°F/Gas 4). Brush a little of the oil over an oven tray and lay the aubergine slices in a single layer on it. Brush the tops of the slices sparingly with the remaining olive oil. Sprinkle them with salt and pepper and bake for 20–25 minutes until soft and lightly golden. Remove from the oven and allow to cool for 15 minutes.

Meanwhile, mix the rest of the ingredients (except the tomato sauce) together in a bowl to form the stuffing. Season to taste and, when the baked aubergines are just warm to the touch, put a tablespoon of the stuffing onto the thin end of each aubergine slice. Roll them up and place them seam side down in a lasagne dish. Spoon a little tomato sauce over each roll and bake for 20 minutes or until the sauce is bubbling hot and just starting to brown. Serve warm with a green salad.

pasta with caffè caldesi sauce

**SERVES
6 PEOPLE**

1 quantity of Homemade
   Tomato Sauce (see page 40)
½ teaspoon dried chilli flakes
3 tablespoons double
   (heavy) cream
salt and freshly ground
   black pepper
480 g (17 oz) dried pasta,
   such as linguine

TO SERVE
good-quality extra-virgin
   olive oil
a few basil leaves
25 g (1 oz) grated Parmesan

The most popular pasta at our restaurant in London, Caffè Caldesi, is Giancarlo's favourite, the Linguine Caldesi. In this case, the tomato sauce on page 40 is given a touch of heat with chilli and then cooled down with double cream, before being stirred into hot linguine. Our children still love it this way, so I often make it with linguine for them and roasted vegetables for us. We often use roasted vegetables as a base for sauces in place of pasta. It makes for a lighter meal at lunchtime and is a really delicious way to eat traditional Italian sauces such tomato or ragù, if you can't eat pasta.

Heat the tomato sauce with the chilli and cream in a frying pan until bubbling and hot. Taste and season, adjusting the heat of the chilli as necessary.

Meanwhile, cook the pasta according to the packet instructions (see page 41 for how to cook dried pasta) and time it so the pasta will be just cooked when the sauce is ready.

Once the sauce is ready, stir in the freshly cooked pasta and serve in warmed bowls. Dress with a swirl of good-quality olive oil, top with a basil leaf, and scatter over the grated Parmesan.

pasta for lunch...

Lunch is the time in Tuscany to eat pasta. In most households you will find pots of ragù or tomato sauce in the fridge for just such a time. We sometimes have a ball of leftover pasta dough in the fridge, so all I need to do is quickly roll it through the pasta machine and drop the strands into boiling water for a couple of minutes to make a quick lunch. However, dried pasta is perfectly acceptable and its quick cooking time makes it perfect for a meal when you have little time for preparation. Many Italians also eat it in the evening, or late into the night, but always in small portions. Giancarlo remembers preparing *un spaghettata* in the early hours of the morning after a night's dancing: he would boil up pasta and serve it with a little chilli, splashes of new olive oil, a handful of chopped parsley and some of the local sheep's cheese. For tips on cooking dried pasta, see page 41.

cheat's spaghetti with clams

**SERVES
4 PEOPLE**

4 tablespoons extra-virgin
    olive oil
400 g (14 oz) tin Italian
    plum tomatoes
280 g (10 oz) tin clams
    in brine, drained
320 g (11½ oz) dried spaghetti

FOR THE BATTUTO
20 g (¾ oz) parsley leaves
    and fine stalks, plus a few
    more leaves, roughly
    chopped, to serve
1 small garlic clove, peeled
salt and freshly ground
    black pepper
fresh red chilli, finely
    chopped, to taste,
    or ¼ teaspoon dried chilli
    flakes

I was shown this cheat's version of a clam sauce one year, which uses a jar of pre-prepared clams in brine, and thought it was delicious, despite being made in just 10 minutes. This sauce works well with spaghetti or linguine. You can also reduce the sauce on the hob and serve it as a topping for polenta crostini (see page 37).

Make a *battuto* with the parsley, garlic, a good pinch of salt, a generous twist of pepper and some chilli by finely chopping them together on a board with a sharp knife (see page 29).

Heat the oil in a large frying pan over a gentle heat, add the *battuto* and fry it for about 3 minutes until the garlic is slightly golden but not burnt. Add the tomatoes and wash the tin out with approximately 100 ml (3½ fl oz/ scant ½ cup) of hot water and stir through. Break them up with a potato masher. Cook for around 20 minutes over a medium heat, adding the drained clams halfway through.

Meanwhile, cook the spaghetti according to the packet instructions (see page 41 for how to cook dried pasta) and time it so the pasta will be just cooked when the sauce is ready.

Tip the freshly cooked and drained spaghetti into the pan and toss to combine. Serve straight away with the parsley leaves.

kale & sausage pasta sauce

**SERVES
6 PEOPLE**

300 g (10½ oz) cavolo nero
  (or other cabbage), washed,
  tough stems removed and
  leaves roughly chopped
6 good-quality (over 90% meat)
  pork sausages
5 tablespoons extra-virgin
  olive oil
2 fat garlic cloves, peeled
  and lightly crushed
fresh red chilli, sliced, to taste,
  or ¼ teaspoon dried chilli
  flakes
480 g (17 oz) dried pasta
3 tablespoons white wine
100 ml (3½ fl oz/scant ½ cup)
  double (heavy) cream
  (optional)
salt and freshly ground
  black pepper
25 g (1 oz) grated Parmesan

If you can, find Italian sausages to give this sauce a more genuine Tuscan taste; however, we frequently make it with good-quality English ones, as long as the meat is coarsely ground and they are not stuffed with rusk. Italian sausages are made with 100 per cent meat, have a good fat content and are flavoured with salt and garlic, and are often used in Italian recipes as sausage meat or instead of minced meat. If you do find them you may not need any extra garlic or salt in the recipe. This recipe comes from Raffaella Cecchelli who runs the smallest osteria in Italy called La Tana dei Brillo Parlante in the stunningly pretty town of Massa Marittima. In the photo we have used fresh papperdele, but this sauce is also ideal with penne, fusilli or rigatoni dried pasta.

Bring a large saucepan of salted water to the boil, add the cavolo nero and cook for 5–10 minutes until soft. Drain well and set aside. When cool enough to touch, cut the leaves into shreds.

Make a shallow incision along the length of the sausages with a knife and peel away the skin. Discard the skins and crumble the meat into a large frying pan, then add the oil, garlic and chilli. Put the pan over a medium heat and cook until the sausage meat is lightly browned, breaking it up with a wooden spoon as it cooks.

Meanwhile, cook the pasta according to the packet instructions (see page 41 for how to cook dried pasta) and time it so the pasta will be just cooked when the sauce is ready.

Add the white wine to the sausage mixture in the frying pan and allow this to evaporate for around 5 minutes, then add the shredded cavolo nero and stir through. Pour in the cream, if using, bring the sauce to a gentle boil and taste for seasoning (sometimes there is no need add more salt if the sausages are already salty). Stir hot, drained pasta into the sauce and serve straight away with the grated Parmesan.

linguine with crab & cream

**SERVES 4 AS A MAIN /
6 AS A STARTER**

3 tablespoons extra-virgin
    olive oil
15 cherry tomatoes, halved
100 g (3½ oz) brown crab meat
    and 300 g (10½ oz) white
    crab meat
100 ml (3½ fl oz/scant ½ cup)
    Prosecco or white wine
4 tablespoons double
    (heavy) cream
320 g (11½ oz) dried linguine

FOR THE BATTUTO
large handful of parsley,
    roughly chopped, plus
    2 tablespoons finely
    chopped
1 garlic clove, peeled
fresh red chilli, finely
    chopped, to taste,
    or ¼ teaspoon dried chilli
    flakes
salt and freshly ground
    black pepper

I always like to buy fresh crab meat when I am by the coast in the UK or Italy. The combination of a little dark meat with the white is superb and gives a richer texture and fuller flavour than the white alone. The strength of the crab can then take the kick of chilli as well as the mellowing effect of the cream. Serve this sauce with dried pasta such as linguine or with fresh tagliatelle.

Make a *battuto* with the 2 tablespoons of parsley, the garlic, chilli, and a pinch of salt and pepper by finely chopping them together on a board with a sharp knife (see page 29).

    Heat the oil in a large frying pan over a low heat and fry the *battuto* for 3 minutes, until the garlic just starts to soften but doesn't burn. Add the cherry tomatoes and crab meat and fry for a couple of minutes. Increase the heat and pour in the Prosecco or white wine and allow it to evaporate for a few minutes until the strong smell of alcohol has gone. Pour in the cream and shake the pan to blend it into the sauce. Taste and season with salt and pepper as necessary. Remove from the heat and set aside.

    Cook the pasta until just al dente. Take 2 tablespoons of water from the pasta saucepan and add it to the sauce in the frying pan. Drain the pasta and put this in too. Add the remaining parsley and toss or stir through briefly. Serve straight away in warmed bowls.

pasta with roasted tomatoes, chilli & garlic

**SERVES 4 AS A MAIN /
6 AS A STARTER**

1 kg (2 lb 3 oz) cherry tomatoes,
    halved around the equator
    (not pole to pole)
7 tablespoons extra-virgin
    olive oil
5 garlic cloves (skin on)
a little fresh red chilli, finely
    sliced, to taste, or
    ¼ teaspoon dried chilli
    flakes
salt and freshly ground
    black pepper
1 quantity of fresh pappardelle
    (see page 168) or 320 g
    (11½ oz) dried pasta
handful of basil leaves,
    roughly torn if large
25 g (1 oz) grated Parmesan

Aglio is garlic in Italian, so *aglione* means 'lots of garlic', referring to the flavour of the dish. Traditionally this sauce is made from peeled plum tomatoes cooked with garlic cloves, served over thick strands of *pici* (see page 181). However, we like our version, which takes very little time to throw together; the tomatoes roast as you prepare the pasta and the combination is heavenly. You can serve the sauce with fresh tagliatelle or pappardelle, or dried shell-shaped pasta is good as it collects the sauce.

Don't be alarmed by the amount of olive oil. This will be the sauce when combined with the sweet juices from the tomatoes and the garlic.

Preheat the oven to 170°C (340°F/Gas 3). Put the tomatoes cut side up in a roasting tray and pour over the oil. Put the garlic cloves between the tomatoes and any tomato stems if you have them, as they will flavour the oil. Scatter with dried chilli (if using – add fresh chilli later on), season with salt and pepper, and roast for 15–20 minutes or until the tomatoes just start to collapse and brown. After 10 minutes stir the fresh chilli (if using fresh instead of dried) into the oil (fresh chilli might burn if put on top of the tomatoes at the beginning).

Meanwhile, cook the pasta to coincide with the end of the cooking time for the tomatoes (see page 41 if using dried pasta).

When the tomatoes are cooked, remove the tray from the oven and use the flat of a wooden spoon to squeeze the soft garlic out of their skins. Mix this gently with the tomatoes and discard the garlic skins as well as the tomato stems. Pour the drained pasta into the hot tray. Add the basil leaves and use a pair of tongs to combine, then serve straight away in warmed bowls, scattered with the Parmesan.

turkey breast stuffed with pecorino & sage alla livia

**SERVES
8 PEOPLE**

1 or 2 turkey breasts, or
    6 escalopes, weighing
    approx. 850 g (1 lb 14 oz)
salt and freshly ground black
    pepper
small bunch of sage leaves
200 g (7 oz) young Pecorino
    or Fontina, cut into
    18 finger-sized pieces
4 tablespoons extra-virgin
    olive oil
100 ml (3½ fl oz/scant ½ cup)
    dry white wine
150 ml (5 fl oz/generous ⅔ cup)
    Chicken or Vegetable Stock
    (see page 32 or 35)

TO SERVE
sautéed spinach or Swiss
    chard (see page 38)
    (optional)
Potatoes & Leeks or Spring
    Onions (see page 224)
    (optional)

Livia is a dear friend of ours who lives on a smallholding with her husband Nello. She invented this dish when we arrived for a spontaneous supper with a selection of Pecorino and all she had were some slices of turkey and plenty of sage in the garden. We loved it and now cook it at home for family suppers. The parcels can be prepared in advance and kept in the fridge, covered, for a day.

Cut the turkey breast into 8 slices around 2 cm (¾ in) thick. Put a piece of turkey between two sheets of cling film (plastic wrap) and use a meat tenderiser or the base of a small pan to bash the meat out until it reaches a thickness of 1 cm (½ in).

Season one side of the turkey with salt and pepper and lay 3 sage leaves over the top, spread out from one another. Put 3 slices of cheese on top. Roll the turkey up, folding the sides in where possible, and secure with a toothpick or two. Repeat for each piece of turkey. You will have to improvise as each piece will be a slightly different shape; some may look like rolls and some like parcels. Don't worry too much about the cheese escaping – it will melt into the sauce anyway. Season each parcel with salt and pepper. Set aside in the fridge until you are ready to cook.

Heat the oil in a large non-stick lidded pan over a medium–high heat. When the oil is hot, put the turkey parcels into the pan. Brown for 5 minutes, uncovered, on each side or until golden. Pour in the wine and stock and bring to the boil. Put the lid on the pan slightly ajar and turn the heat to medium. Cook for 10 minutes, then turn the parcels. Put the lid on ajar again and cook for a further 10 minutes. Pierce the parcels with a skewer to make sure the juices run clear and not pink.

Remove the parcels from the pan and keep warm. Boil the juices down until reduced to about 150 ml (5 fl oz). Serve with the juices from the pan, sautéed spinach or swiss chard, and the Potatoes & Leeks or Spring Onions on page 224.

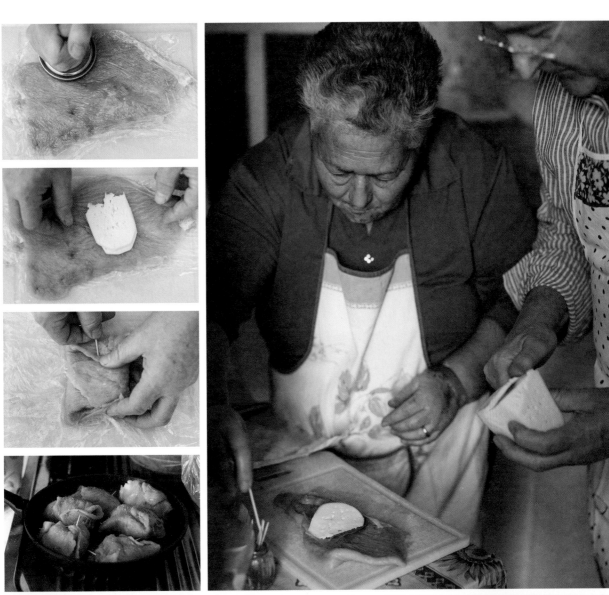

fricassee of chicken with sage & onions

This recipe has been passed through the generations on Giancarlo's side. Originally it was cooked in a cauldron over the fire. The sauce is thickened with egg yolks and lemon at the end of the cooking time, which gives a rich, creamy finish to the dish without the use of cream.

**SERVES
6 PEOPLE**

6 chicken thighs, bone-in
and skin on
12 large sage leaves
salt and freshly ground
black pepper
2 tablespoons extra-virgin
olive oil or chicken fat
2 sprigs of rosemary
2 garlic cloves, peeled
and lightly crushed
4 slices of unsmoked bacon,
roughly chopped
1 white onion, sliced into
half-moons
100 ml (3½ fl oz/scant ½ cup)
white wine
600 ml (7 fl oz/generous ¾ cup)
hot chicken stock (see page
32) or hot water
2 egg yolks
juice of 1 lemon

TO SERVE
Potatoes & Leeks or Spring
Onions (see page 224),

Peel back the skin on the chicken thighs and push a large sage leaf underneath each one. Replace the skin over the leaves. Season the chicken thighs all over with salt and pepper.

Heat the oil or chicken fat in a large heavy-based frying pan with a lid. Add the chicken thighs to the pan skin side down, along with the rosemary and garlic, and fry the chicken for 15–20 minutes until it is golden and crisp. Turn the chicken thighs over, add the bacon and onion, and fry until the bacon is lightly browned and the onion is soft.

Pour in the white wine and allow to reduce for around 5 minutes, then add a third of the stock or hot water. Bring to the boil, then reduce the heat to a gentle simmer. Cook, partially covered, for 30–40 minutes or until the meat is cooked through and falls easily from the bones. During the cooking time, keep the level of the liquid topped up with the remaining stock so that it doesn't dry out. You should be left with around 200 ml (7 fl oz/scant 1 cup) of liquid left in the pan for the sauce. Roughly chop the rest of the sage leaves and add them to the pan around 10 minutes before the end of cooking time.

Whisk the egg yolks and lemon juice together in a small bowl. Move the chicken pieces to one side of the pan so that the juices collect together in a pool on the other side. Turn the heat to very low. Gradually add the egg mixture to the pan to thicken the sauce (you may not need to use all of it). Move the chicken around the pan to distribute the sauce and serve straight away. Serve with the Potatoes & Leeks or Spring Onions on page 224.

POTATOES &
LEEKS OR
SPRING ONIONS
(PAGE 224)

giancarlo's tuscan chicken with rosemary & garlic

**SERVES
4 PEOPLE**

8 chicken thighs, bone in
and skin on
salt and freshly ground
black pepper
8 short sprigs of rosemary
8 garlic cloves, skin on
and lightly crushed
4 tablespoons extra-virgin
olive oil
100 ml (3½ fl oz/scant ½ cup)
white wine

This is a family favourite as it is really simple to make, everyone loves it and it can be left in the oven to cook while you get on with something else. It doesn't have to be made from thighs – a jointed chicken also works well. The chicken is also delicious cold and served sliced in a *panino* with mayonnaise.

Preheat the oven to 180°C (350°F/Gas 4) and line a baking tray with baking parchment. Season the chicken thighs generously all over with salt and pepper. Lay the rosemary and garlic in the baking tray and put the chicken thighs on top, skin side up. Drizzle over the oil and put the chicken in the oven for 30 minutes, then splash the white wine around the chicken but not onto the crispy skin. Return the chicken to the oven and bake for a further 20–30 minutes or until cooked through and the meat falls from the bones (the cooking time will depend on the size of the thighs). Serve with roast potatoes or salad on a separate plate.

rabbit casserole

**SERVES
6 PEOPLE**

5 tablespoons extra-virgin
    olive oil
1 large red onion, peeled
    and roughly chopped
1.6 kg (2 lb 5 oz) rabbit
    (1 medium rabbit), jointed
    into 12 pieces
1½ teaspoons salt
freshly ground black pepper
1 rabbit liver (optional)
200 ml (7 fl oz/generous
    ¾ cup) dry white wine
2 heaped tablespoons
    tomato purée (paste)
400 ml (13 fl oz/1¾ cups)
    Chicken or Vegetable Stock
    (see page 32 or 35), or water
80 g (3 oz) black olives
    (stones in)

TO SERVE
Swiss chard or spinach
    (see page 38)

Our friends Clare and Mirko live in rural Tuscany and learnt this recipe from their neighbour. Rabbits are either farmed or shot in the wild. Giancarlo tells me they are always sold with the head on so that you know you are not buying a cat, as was once the way in poorer days. As rabbit usually comes with the liver in Italy, this is either added to the dish or dusted in flour, fried briefly and given to children. You can also add the liver to a meat ragù (see page 171). The recipe works equally well with chicken.

Heat the oil in a large, wide casserole or heavy-based pan over a low heat. Add the onion and cook for about 10 minutes until soft. Add the rabbit and season them with the salt and a few good twists of pepper. Cook over a low-medium heat for about 20 minutes, turning the meat occasionally, until the pieces of meat are golden all over. Keep an eye on the pan as you don't want the onions to burn. Roughly chop the liver and add it to the pan, if you have it, followed by the wine, and leave to simmer gently for about 20 minutes.

Stir the tomato purée into the stock or water, then pour it into the pan. Continue to cook for about 40 minutes, or until the meat is soft and falling from the bones. At the last moment, add the olives.

Remove from the heat and serve with Swiss chard or spinach drizzled with your best olive oil and some lemon juice.

●

Variation: Chicken casserole
Use 1 chicken, jointed into 12 pieces, instead of Rabbit.

●

porcini risotto

We loved this recipe when we ate it at our friend Gary Marshall's house. Gary makes a small quantity because, being from Italian descent, he only ever eats it as a starter. To make it a main meal, double the recipe. 'Make sure it is sizzling,' he says, as you should hear a risotto not just see it. Keep tasting it so that you get the seasoning right and have a feel for when the rice grains are done. Keep the pan hot, or the stock doesn't boil off. My preferred risotto rice is carnaroli. It is a lot more forgiving than arborio as it is less absorbent and therefore less likely to make the risotto sticky.

**SERVES
6 AS A STARTER / 4 AS A MAIN**

50 g (2 oz) dried porcini mushrooms
500 ml (17 fl oz/2¼ cups) warm water
500 g (1 lb 2 oz) portobello or chestnut mushrooms, roughly chopped
4 tablespoons extra-virgin olive oil
1 fat garlic clove, peeled and lightly crushed
1 sprig of rosemary
3 sprigs of thyme
approx. 600 ml (20 fl oz/ 2½ cups) Chicken or Vegetable Stock (see page 32 or 35)
50 g (2 oz) salted butter
1 medium leek, finely chopped
1 small white onion, finely chopped
1 celery stalk, finely chopped
150 g (5 oz/generous ⅔ cups) carnaroli rice
150 ml (5 fl oz/generous ⅔ cup) white wine
25 g (1 oz) grated Parmesan
salt and freshly ground black pepper
small handful of parsley, finely chopped

Soak the porcini mushrooms in a bowl with the warm water for 15–20 minutes. Remove the porcini mushrooms from the water with a slotted spoon, saving the soaking water for later, and coarsely chop them on a board, then add them to the chopped portobello mushrooms. Pass the mushroom soaking water through a piece of paper towel in a sieve into a separate bowl, to remove any sediment.

Heat 2 tablespoons of the oil with the garlic, rosemary and thyme in a large heavy-based frying pan over a medium heat until you can smell the garlic. Add the mushrooms and fry for 5–7 minutes, until soft. Transfer the mushrooms to a plate and set aside, and discard the rosemary and thyme (leave the garlic in). Don't wash the pan. Warm the stock in a saucepan over a medium heat.

Meanwhile, gently heat the rest of the oil and half the butter in the frying pan you used for cooking the mushrooms over a low heat. When hot, add the leek, onion and celery, and fry for about 10 minutes until softened. Increase the heat to medium, add the rice to the pan and allow it to crackle and toast for a few minutes, stirring constantly with a wooden spoon. Add the cooked mushrooms to the pan and stir through, then pour in the wine. Bring to the boil and cook for 5–7 minutes, stirring, until the wine is absorbed by the rice. Add a few ladlefuls of the warm stock and stir with a wooden spoon. Continue adding more stock as each addition gets absorbed. After 20–25 minutes, the rice grains should be almost transparent and have just a slight crunch in the middle. Remove the pan from the heat, making sure the consistency of the risotto is loose and not cloying. It should move easily – in Italy they call this *al onda* (like a wave).

Add the remaining butter and the Parmesan and stir through with vigour – this stage is called *mantecare* and your effort is rewarded when the risotto becomes creamy as the starch breaks down. Taste and adjust the seasoning as necessary. Cover the pan for no more than 3 minutes. Spoon the risotto into warmed bowls and serve scattered with parsley.

pheasant & leek risotto

**SERVES
6 PEOPLE**

approx. 1.2 litres (2 pints/
    5 cups) Pheasant Stock
    (see page 35)
2 tablespoons extra-virgin
    olive oil
75 g (3 oz) butter
½ large leek, finely chopped
1 celery stalk, finely diced
300 g (10½ oz) carnaroli rice
2 sprigs of thyme
150 ml (5 fl oz/⅔ cup)
    white wine
200–250 g (7–9 oz) cooked
    pheasant meat left over
    from cooking the stock
salt and freshly ground
    black pepper
35 g (1¼ oz) grated Parmesan

This risotto makes the most of the glorious flavours of a game stock. Pheasants are easy to buy in season but can be dry to roast. Here, the bird is poached as the stock is being made to ensure the meat remains tender. Other game birds can be used in the same way and the leek can be substituted for a white onion.

Warm the stock in a saucepan over a medium heat. Meanwhile, heat the oil and half the butter in a large heavy-based frying pan over a low heat. When hot, add the leek and the celery, and cook for 10–15 minutes until softened but not browned. Increase the heat to medium and add the rice and thyme. Allow the rice to crackle and toast, stirring constantly with a wooden spoon for a few minutes before pouring in the wine. Bring to the boil and cook for 5–7 minutes, stirring, until the wine is absorbed. Remove the thyme sprigs. Add a few ladlefuls of warm stock and stir through with a wooden spoon. Continue adding more stock as each edition gets absorbed.

Add the pheasant meat to the pan after the rice has been cooking for about 15 minutes, and continue cooking for 5–10 minutes. The rice is ready when the rice grains are almost transparent. Taste it regularly to test for doneness and season to taste. When the rice has just a slight crunch in the middle, remove the pan from the heat, making sure the consistency of the risotto is loose and not cloying. It should move easily. Add the remaining butter and Parmesan and stir through with gusto to break down the starch until the risotto becomes creamy. Cover the pan for no more than 3 minutes while you prepare warmed bowls. Serve with a twist of black pepper.

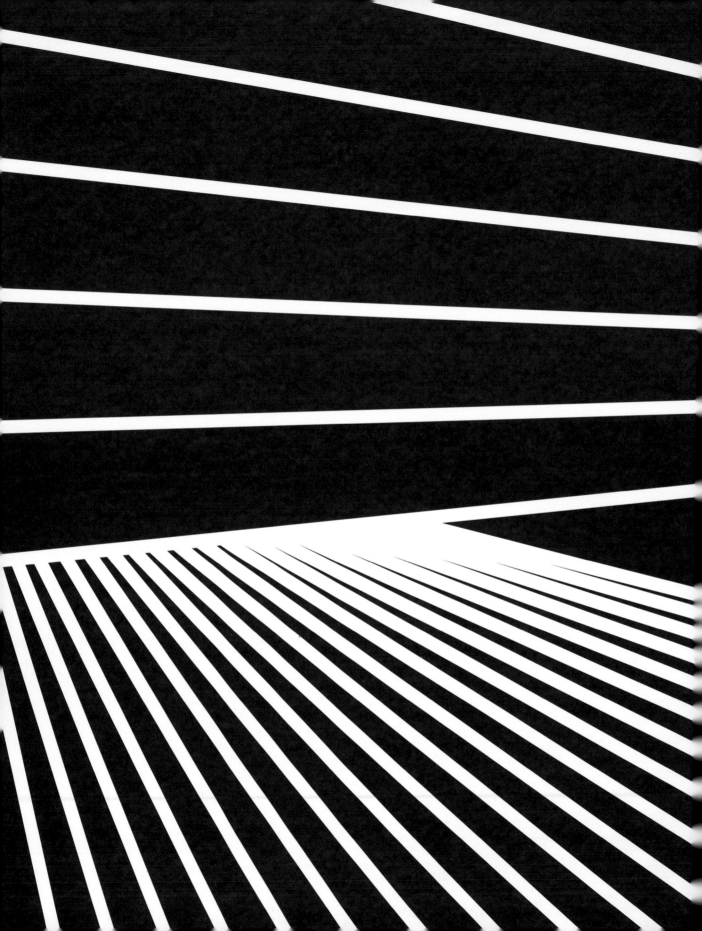

aperitivo

aperitivo hour

This is one of our favourite times of the day; the magic hour when twilight comes, people start to leave work and once again the bars are crowded with Italians stopping off for a quick Aperol spritz or Prosecco and a bite before heading home for supper. Italians call it *aperitivo*, which will last all but a few hours when you pay a hefty price for a cocktail but are then given a plate and told to help yourself to an array of antipasti or small bites at the bar. These vary in quality, so do pick your bar carefully. Here are our favourite antipasti, from the range we have discovered in bars and in Tuscan homes on our travels. The bases can be switched: instead of toasted bread, you could try the polenta slices on page 37, or try the chicken liver pâté from page 119 on the Chickpea Pancake on page 126.

cheese & mixed seed cantuccini

**MAKES
APPROX. 35 CANTUCCINI**

olive oil, for greasing
125 g (4 oz/1 cup) '00', plain
    (all-purpose) or gluten-free
    flour, plus 1 tablespoon to
    coat the loaves
50 g (2 oz) grated Parmesan
75 g (2½ oz) Gorgonzola Dolce,
    including the rind
100 g (3½ oz) salted butter
75 g (2½ oz/scant ¾ cup)
    ground almonds
    (almond meal)
1 teaspoon baking powder
1 egg, plus 1 egg yolk
pinch of salt
pinch of freshly ground
    black pepper
35 g (1¼ oz) mixed seeds, such
    as pumpkin, sunflower and
    sesame
15 g (½ oz) black onion seeds
25 g (1 oz) walnuts
1 tablespoon pink peppercorns

TO SERVE
cream cheese
basil leaves
cherry tomatoes, halved

These rustic and incredibly moreish biscuits are wonderful on their own as a snack, spread with ricotta or cream cheese and topped with halved cherry tomatoes and basil leaves to go with drinks, or served warm with a bowl of hot soup. They keep for a week or so in an airtight container so have them on standby during the festive season.

Preheat the oven to 170°C (340°F/Gas 3) and lightly grease a baking tray with oil. Put the flour, cheeses, butter, ground almonds, baking powder, egg, egg yolk and seasoning in a food processor and blitz until well combined. Add the seeds, walnuts and peppercorns, and give the mixture a quick blitz to combine and roughly chop them. The mixture doesn't need to be completely smooth – it is good to have a little texture from the nuts.

Divide the dough in half and roll each piece into a long sausage around 25 × 5 cm (10 × 2 in). Put them on the greased baking tray and lightly flatten them so that they look like a slightly squashed salami. Bake for 20–25 minutes or until just golden. Remove from the oven and set aside to rest for 5 minutes.

Use a cake slice to move the rolls to a chopping board and cut them at a diagonal angle into 1 cm- (½ in-) thick slices. Move these back onto the tray – they can be standing upright and spaced apart or lying down – and bake again for 15–20 minutes or until they are firm to the touch and lightly browned.

Remove from the oven and allow to cool. They will keep in an airtight container for up to 1 week. Serve topped with cream cheese, fresh basil and half a cherry tomato.

toasted bread topped with chicken liver pâté

**MAKES
10–15 CROSTINI**

100 ml (3½ fl oz/scant ½ cup)
    extra-virgin olive oil
1 small red onion,
    finely chopped
8 sage leaves, roughly
    chopped
300 g (10½ oz) chicken livers
salt and freshly ground
    black pepper
100 ml (3½ fl oz/scant ½ cup)
    white wine or Vin Santo
50 g (2 oz) capers in salt,
    well rinsed

TO SERVE
1 country-style loaf
approx 2–3 tablespoons
    room-temperature
    Chicken Stock (see page 32)
    to dip the bread in
small handful of freshly
    chopped sage (optional)

When our good friend Giancarlo Barbafieri's cook, Daniela, kills a chicken they keep the liver in the freezer. When she has collected enough chicken livers she makes this pâté. This *crostini con patè* is made differently all over Tuscany. In my husband Giancarlo's area, the crostini are called *crostini neri*, meaning 'little black toasts', and Vin Santo is added instead of white wine for a sweet touch. Some people add anchovies and leave out the salt; others hand chop the livers with the capers for a coarse finish (you can pulse them in a food processor if you wish). Daniela showed me a trick to soften the bread a little: she dipped each crostini in stock before topping it with pâté. A little fresh sage on top was a lovely addition by our son, Giorgio.

Heat the oil in a medium non-stick frying pan over a low heat. Add the onion and roughly chopped sage. Cook for around 10 minutes or until the onion is soft. Meanwhile, prepare the chicken livers by removing the tough connective tissue. Add the livers and seasoning and stir until they are browned all over. Pour in the wine or Vin Santo and continue to cook for 15–20 minutes until the liquid has reduced by half and the livers are cooked through.

Put the mixture into a food processor with the capers and blend to a rough or smooth consistency, depending on how you like it. Taste and season again as necessary.

To serve, make the crostini: preheat the oven to 180°C (350°F/Gas 4). Cut the bread into 1.5 cm- (½ in-) thick slices and lay them on a baking tray. Bake in the oven for around 5 minutes until lightly golden brown and crisp. Cut the bread into canape-sized pieces and dip one side of each piece briefly into a saucer of stock, then top with the pâté. (The bread shouldn't become soggy – the stock just softens it a little as often slightly stale bread is used.) Scatter over the finely chopped sage (if using) and serve straight away.

TOASTED
BREAD WITH
TOMATO &
CLAM SAUCE
(PAGE 122)

TOASTED
BREAD WITH
MOZZARELLA
& PORCINI
MUSHROOMS
(PAGE 125)

TOASTED
BREAD WITH
GREEN SAUCE
(PAGE 123)

TOASTED
BREAD TOPPED
WITH CHICKEN
LIVER PÂTÉ
(PAGE 119)

CHEESE
& MIXED SEED
CANTUCCINI
(PAGE 118)

toasted bread with tomato & clam sauce

**SERVES
8 PEOPLE**

½ quantity of tomato and
   clam sauce (see page 97)

TO SERVE
16 small slices of bread
   from a baguette
small handful of parsley,
   roughly chopped

**This is a good way to use up the tomato and clam sauce on page 97.
It makes a delicious seafood-flavour canapé and goes down very well
with a glass of Prosecco.**

Put the clam sauce in a saucepan over a medium heat and let it reduce until
it is dense and more like a spread than a sauce – around 20 minutes should
do it. To serve, toast the bread as in the recipe for Toasted Bread Topped with
Chicken Liver Pâté on page 119. Top the bread with the sauce (there is no need
to dip it in the stock this time). Garnish each one with a little parsley and serve
straight away.

toasted bread with green sauce

**SERVES
12 PEOPLE**

30 g (1 oz) parsley leaves,
    stalks discarded
1 small garlic clove, peeled
2 anchovy fillets
1 tablespoon capers, well
    rinsed
1 teaspoon red or white
    wine vinegar
4 tablespoons extra-virgin
    olive oil
salt and freshly ground black
    pepper

TO SERVE
12 small slices of bread from
    a baguette
50 g (2 oz) unsalted butter

Do look out for salted anchovies in Italian delis. They have a strong umami flavour with a bite that pairs brilliantly with the buttered toast.

To make the salsa verde, finely chop the parsley, garlic, anchovy fillets and capers together by hand on a board. This is like making a *battuto*, as described on page 29. Put the chopped ingredients into a bowl with the vinegar and olive oil and add seasoning to taste.

    To serve, toast the bread under a hot grill on both sides. Allow to cool, then spread generously with the butter. Spread a little salsa verde onto each one. They will keep in a cool place for up to 1 hour.

toasted bread with mozzarella & porcini mushrooms

This is a great vegetarian canapé with full-on flavour from the porcini mushrooms.

**SERVES
6 PEOPLE**

12 small slices of bread from a baguette
3 tablespoons extra-virgin olive oil
⅓ quantity of cooked chopped mushrooms from the Porcini & Chestnut Mushroom Loaf (see page 205)
2 × 125 g (4 oz) balls of buffalo mozzarella, each cut into 6 × 5 mm (¼ in) slices
handful of torn basil leaves
freshly ground black pepper

Preheat the oven to 180°C (350°F/Gas 4). Bake the bread slices in the oven on a rack (so that both sides are exposed to the heat) for 5 minutes. Remove from the oven and brush with the oil when cool enough to touch. Spread with the mushroom mixture. Top each one with a slice of mozzarella and transfer to a baking tray. Put back in oven for 5 minutes or until the cheese has melted. Remove from the oven and top with a torn basil leaf and a sprinkling of black pepper. Serve straight away.

chickpea pancake

SERVES
8 PEOPLE

150 g (5 oz/1⅔ cups) chickpea (gram) flour

500 ml (17 fl oz/2¼ cups) cold water

1 teaspoon salt

¼ teaspoon freshly ground black pepper, plus extra to serve

2 tablespoons extra-virgin olive oil

1 sprig of rosemary, leaves picked

50 g (2 oz) Pecorino, ricotta, Brie or Camembert, thinly sliced, to serve (optional)

The batter for this pancake needs to be made three hours before it is used. During this time the flour soaks up the water. It is often served with freshly ground black pepper, chopped rosemary and fresh Pecorino or ricotta, Brie or Camembert on top. It is a useful gluten-free recipe for those in need.

Line a 25 cm (10 in) tart tin with baking parchment. Put the flour, water, salt, ¼ teaspoon of pepper and the oil into a large bowl and whisk, either by hand or using an electric mixer. Cover with cling film (plastic wrap) and leave to rest at room temperature for 3 hours.

Preheat the oven to 180°C (350°F/Gas 4). Pour the *cecina* batter into the prepared tin and scatter over the rosemary leaves, discarding the stem. Bake in the oven for around 50 minutes, or until the top is golden brown and starting to crisp. Remove the pancake from the oven and allow it to rest for 5 minutes before removing it from the tin and peeling off the paper. Top with some more black pepper and thinly sliced cheese, if using, then serve warm, cut into triangles.

eating cheese the tuscan way

My first experience of Tuscan family food was with Giancarlo's *Zia* (aunt), Agnese, who showed me how to eat slivers of Pecorino drizzled with honey and slices of peeled ripe pears. It was a combination I will never forget and now in our restaurants we serve Pecorino on wooden boards with pears, honey, walnuts, celery and grapes, mixing the sweet and salty flavours together. In this way, the selection makes a great *antipasto* with drinks, or works in place of a dessert.

Pecorino cheese-making, from the word *pecora*, meaning 'sheep', dates back to Etruscan times when it was made with vegetable rennet, sometimes derived from artichoke flowers until the Sardinian farmers arrived and brought with them techniques for using animal rennet. You will find a huge selection of Pecorino in Pienza, which has DOP status. It is fascinating to try cheeses covered in ash, wrapped in walnut leaves or washed with wine.

Our favourite selection of Tuscan cheeses to serve together would be a young (*fresco*) Pecorino; an older, more mature Pecorino known as Stagionato; a freshly made sheep's ricotta and a soft goat's cheese from Mugello. All of these go with runny honey of varying strengths, from the mild, delicate acacia to the powerful, farmyard-flavoured chestnut honey. Our friend Antonella Secciani told us to try soft goat's cheese with cocoa powder and chestnut honey. And you will often see cheeses served with a soft-set sweet marmalade as well as more modern chilli jam.

dinner

dinner

La cena is eaten at home or out at a restaurant. It is usually a lighter and quieter affair during the week and builds up to a family- or friend-filled feast at the weekend. Here we have included recipes that take a little longer to prepare for family suppers, entertaining and weekend eating. Dinner begins with *primi*, meaning 'first', which consists of soup, a light starter, pasta or gnocchi (see pages 136–83). *Secondi* follows, with meat, fish or vegetarian main courses (see pages 184–213), all served with vegetables or salad, *contorni* (see pages 215–37).

-

soups & starters ¹³⁶
pasta & gnocchi ¹⁶¹
secondi ¹⁸⁴

soups
& starters

La cucina povera, 'the poor kitchen' diet, prevailed among the rural population for centuries and made good use of food leftovers, with *ribollita* ('re-boiled') featuring prominently. This variety of Tuscan soup with peasant origins was made by re-boiling vegetables left over from the previous day, and dates back to the Middle Ages, when servants gathered up food such as soaked bread trenchers from the banquets of their feudal masters and re-boiled them for their own dinners.

A *zuppa* (from *inzuppare*, meaning 'to soak') is a soup usually served over bread. A *minestra* is made from vegetables, and could be thin or thickened with potato. Bean soups are ubiquitous, and the Florentines in particular were always known as the *mangiafagioli* ('beaneaters'). A *crema* is a soup that has been passed through a food mill to make it creamy and smooth.

Our best-selling *primo* at our restaurant Caldesi in Campagna is the *torta di grana*, a wonderfully light cheese tart. It is similar to the *sformati* ('moulds') that are served either as *primi* or *contorni* with main courses. The Cibreo (braised chicken livers, see 155) dates back to the time of Catherine de' Medici and is said to have been one of her favourite dishes.

farro soup with prawns

**SERVES
4 PEOPLE**

FOR THE SOFFRITTO
1 medium carrot
1 celery stalk
1 medium white onion
5 tablespoons extra-virgin
   olive oil, plus extra for
   drizzling
freshly ground black pepper
red chilli, to taste, finely
   chopped (optional)
1 bay leaf
1 garlic clove, peeled and
   crushed with the flat side
   of a knife but left whole
6 thick parsley stalks, very
   finely chopped

FOR THE SOUP
250 g (9 oz) farro
1.2 litres (2 pints/5 cups) warm
   Prawn Stock (see page 34)
2 heaped tablespoons
   tomato purée (paste)
2 level teaspoons salt
freshly ground black pepper,
   to taste
4 large whole raw prawns
   (shrimp)

The idea for this soup came from Pino di Cicco at his restaurant Antica Osteria Da Divo in Siena, where a plump peeled prawn (shrimp) sat curled on top of a warm bath of soup. Giancarlo couldn't try it as it contains gluten, so I tried to conceal how good it was, but he realised when I ate the very last grain of spelt from the bottom of the bowl that he was missing something really quite special! You can make this soup with quick-cook farro dicocco, in which case cut the cooking time down to 10 minutes once you add the grains. To make it gluten-free, you could use brown basmati rice or quinoa instead, but alter the cooking times accordingly.

Make and cook the *soffritto* (see page 28). Add the farro and cook for about 5 minutes, stirring frequently, so that it absorbs the juices from the *soffritto*. Add 1 litre (34 fl oz/4¼ cups) of the stock and the tomato purée and bring to the boil. Reduce the heat and simmer for 20–25 minutes or until the farro is cooked. Add a little more stock or water if the soup looks too thick. Taste the grains to check if they are soft; when they are, your soup is done. Season to taste with salt and a few generous twists of pepper. If you are making it in advance the grains will continue to swell so when you reheat, simply add more hot stock or hot water as necessary to achieve a thick soup consistency.

While the farro is cooking, prepare the shellfish. Remove the heads from the prawns and peel off the shells (don't throw them away – freeze them for making prawn stock – see page 34). Cut a thin incision along their backs and extract the black veins.

Put a quarter of the soup in a blender or through a *passatutto* (food mill) and return it to the pan. Add the peeled prawns and simmer for about 15 minutes or until the shellfish is cooked through. Divide the soup between 4 bowls, sit a prawn on top of each serving and drizzle with a swirl of good extra-virgin olive oil.

winter tomato & bread soup

**SERVES
8 PEOPLE**

100 ml (3½ fl oz/scant ½ cup)
    extra-virgin olive oil
8 small sage leaves
4 small garlic cloves, peeled
    and roughly chopped
1 teaspoon salt
freshly ground black pepper
2 × 400 g (14 oz) tins whole
    plum tomatoes, or 800 g
    (1 lb 12 oz) Fresh Tomato
    Passata (see page 41)
250 g (9 oz) stale bread, crusts
    removed and cut into
    approx. 3 cm (1¼ in) cubes
1 litre (34 fl oz/4¼ cups)
    Chicken or Vegetable Stock
    (see page 32 or 35)
15 large basil or mint leaves

Pappa al pomodoro **always contains a huge amount of olive oil.
Don't stint on this, as it just won't be the same velvety rich soup without
it. The soup is thickened with the saltless Tuscan bread. This is hard to
get outside Tuscany, so you can use a robust white country loaf instead.
Test a little bread first to see how it behaves in the soup – not all bread
works well: sourdough is too strong in flavour and some white bread
becomes cloying. Chef Daniela, at the hilltop *agriturismo* La Mandriola,
makes this soup all year round, swapping mint for basil when she has
it. This is her winter version, which uses passata or tinned tomatoes.
In summer you can make passata using the recipe on page 41.** *Pappa
al pomodoro* **should always be served lukewarm, not hot.**

Heat the oil in a large saucepan with the sage and garlic over a low heat
for a couple of minutes. Add the salt and a twist of pepper followed by the
tomatoes. Mash the tomatoes in the pan with a potato masher. Add the bread
and stock to the pan and stir through. Cook the soup for up to 30 minutes,
stirring frequently with a wooden spoon and letting it bubble away slowly until
the bread has softened and broken down into the soup. Taste and adjust the
seasoning. Remove from the heat, stir in the basil or mint leaves and allow
to cool a little before serving.

winter soup

SERVES
6–8 PEOPLE

FOR THE SOFFRITTO
6 tablespoons extra-virgin
    olive oil
1 medium carrot,
    finely chopped
1 large red or white onion,
    peeled and finely chopped
1 large celery stalk,
    finely chopped
2 garlic cloves, peeled
    and lightly squashed
1–2 teaspoons salt
freshly ground black pepper,
    to taste
large handful of parsley,
    finely chopped
1 sprig of rosemary (optional)

FOR THE SOUP
250 g (9 oz) potatoes, cut into
    2 cm (¾ in) dice
250 g (9 oz) white cabbage,
    shredded
400 g (14 oz) raw cavolo nero
    leaves, roughly chopped
75 g (2½ oz) curly kale, tough
    stalks removed and leaves
    roughly chopped (optional)
1 litre (34 fl oz/4¼ cups) warm
    Chicken Stock (see page 32),
    plus 250 ml (8½ fl oz/1 cup)
    bean cooking water or more
    stock
250 g (9 oz) cooked cannellini
    beans (see page 44 for how
    to cook them if using dried)

TO SERVE
6 large slices Tuscan-style
    crusty bread
1 garlic clove, peeled
6–8 spring onions (scallions),
    roughly chopped (optional)
good-quality olive oil

This is a winter minestrone made with the dark, robust leaves of cavolo nero, a native Tuscan kale. We had this soup with our friend, Franca Buonamici, from Lucca and drank it with the neighbour's homemade red wine. It was a wonderful combination and quite touching to know that it dates back centuries.

Using three different cabbages is not strictly necessary but you would be surprised how their flavours differ. The white cabbage is quite sweet against the bitter kales. This is a dish that can change completely according to what vegetables you have available, what is growing in your *orto* or what you have in the back of the fridge (you can add the chopped leftover vegetables from a stock into the soup, too – nothing goes to waste in a Tuscan kitchen). The soup can be eaten after cooking but traditionally it is left for a day then layered with saltless spongy Tuscan bread and cooked again. It is often served with a spring onion (scallion): I find this a little overpowering, but the choice is yours!

Cook all the *soffritto* ingredients for the soup base together for 10–15 minutes in a large stock pot over a low heat until soft (see page 28). Add the potatoes and shredded white cabbage and cook over a medium heat until the cabbage starts to wilt. Add the cavolo nero and kale to the dish and stir through.

Pour in the stock and bring to the boil, turn the heat down to a simmer and cook for 30 minutes, or until the vegetables are cooked through. Divide the cannellini beans in half and add one half to the soup. Purée the other half with a stick blender, then add this to the soup too. Cook for a further 10 minutes or so to warm the beans through. Taste and season as necessary. If desired, serve straight away, or let the soup cool before transferring to the fridge if keeping overnight.

If you are serving the soup in the traditional Tuscan way, preheat the oven to 180°C (350°F/Gas 4). Toast the bread until lightly crisp, then rub each slice with the garlic clove. Pour a layer of the soup into an ovenproof serving bowl, top with a few slices of bread followed by another layer of soup. Repeat until the bread and soup is used up. Cook in the oven for 20–30 minutes or until the soup is piping hot and the bread has soaked up the juices. Serve warm with spring onions, if using, and a swirl of your best olive oil.

pheasant soup

**SERVES
6–8 PEOPLE**

3 tablespoons extra-virgin
   olive oil or chicken fat
1 shallot, peeled and finely
   chopped
1 celery stalk, finely chopped
1 teaspoon salt
freshly ground black pepper
300 g (10½ oz) potatoes,
   peeled and cut into
   1 cm (½ in) dice
220–250 g (8–9 oz) pheasant
   meat leftover from making
   the Pheasant Stock (see
   page 35), roughly torn into
   bite-sized pieces
6 juniper berries, finely
   crushed in a pestle
   and mortar
100 ml (3½ fl oz/scant ½ cup)
   white wine
1.5 litres (2½ pints/6½ cups)
   Pheasant Stock
   (see page 35)
3 tablespoons double
   (heavy) cream
120 g (4 oz) cooked and peeled
   chestnuts, crumbled
good-quality extra-virgin
   olive oil, to serve

Game birds are hunted in season in the Tuscan woods and have been a part of the diet since Etruscan days. This is full of woodsy flavour and we love the contrast of textures of the smooth soup with the crumbly chestnuts. The finished soup is thick and works brilliantly if poured into one side of a shallow bowl with the Creamy Bean Soup on page 146 poured into the other side (see picture opposite).

Heat the oil or fat in a large saucepan over a low heat. Add the shallot and celery, and fry gently for about 10 minutes or until soft and translucent. Add the salt and some pepper with the diced potato, 150 g (5 oz) of the pheasant meat and the crushed juniper berries, and stir through. Fry for a few minutes, then add the wine and stock. Bring to the boil, reduce the heat and simmer for around 30 minutes until the potato is soft.

Remove from the heat and blend with a stick blender, then add the cream, the remaining meat and the chestnuts, reserving a few for decoration.

Bring the soup back to a gentle simmer and taste again for seasoning. The soup should be thick and creamy. If it is too thin for your liking continue to cook and reduce it for up to 30 minutes. Serve warm with a twist of black pepper, the remaining chestnuts and a swirl of olive oil.

CREAMY
BEAN SOUP
(PAGE 146)

PHEASANT
SOUP
(PAGE 144)

creamy bean soup

**SERVES
6 PEOPLE**

1 quantity of cooked Soffritto
   for 6–8 (see page 28)
250 g (9 oz) dried borlotti
   beans, soaked in cold
   water overnight
2 bay leaves
1 sprig of sage
2 garlic cloves, peeled
   lightly crushed
1–2 level teaspoons salt,
   to taste
freshly ground black pepper
1 Parmesan rind (optional)
small piece of prosciutto
   or unsmoked pancetta
   rind (optional)
5 litres (8¾ pints/21 cups)
   warm Vegetable or Chicken
   Stock (see page 35 or 32),
   or hot water
½ small red onion, peeled
   and finely sliced (optional)
good-quality extra-virgin
   olive oil, to serve

I was asked by a few Tuscan women just before I was about to marry one of their own kin if I knew how to make a bean soup. They were very serious and began to give me instructions, as they felt my new husband would be asking for it twice a week and I had better be able to provide it! Ah, how different things are in the UK – this is Giancarlo's recipe that he cooks for me! For more tips on cooking beans, see page 44. We usually have a Parmesan rind or two in the fridge and sometimes a piece of an end of prosciutto or pancetta, which we add to soups – they are all natural flavour enhancers and are often added to Italian soups.

Spoon the *soffritto* into a large stock pot and add the drained borlotti beans, bay leaves, sage, garlic, 1 teaspoon of salt, a generous twist of pepper, and the Parmesan and prosciutto rinds (if using). Put the pan over a gentle heat and add the stock or hot water. Bring to the boil, then reduce the heat to a simmer. Cook, uncovered, for 1½–2 hours or until the beans are cooked through and soft to the bite.

Remove the bay leaves, sage, and Parmesan and prosciutto rinds (if using) with a slotted spoon. Purée the beans in a food processor or with a stick blender and season to taste.

Soak the onion, if using, in cold water for 15 minutes to make them less potent, drain and dry. Serve a few pieces of onion on top of each bowl of soup with a swirl of olive oil and a twist of black pepper.

●

Variation: Quick Bean Soup
To make a quick bean soup from tinned beans, follow the instructions above but add 750 g (1 lb 10½ oz) cooked and drained beans instead of the soaked beans to the *soffritto* and only 1 litre (34 fl oz/4¼ cups) of stock or hot water. Bring to the boil, then reduce the heat and let the soup simmer for 30 minutes. Remove the bay leaves, sage, and Parmesan and prosciutto rinds (if using), and blend as above.

●

pea & tarragon soup

SERVES
4 PEOPLE

6 tablespoons extra-virgin
    olive oil, plus extra to serve
1 white onion, peeled and
    finely chopped
salt and freshly ground
    black pepper
500 g (1 lb 2 oz) frozen
    or fresh peas
small bunch of tarragon
1 litre (34 fl oz/4¼ cups)
    Chicken Stock (see page 32)
4 slices of pancetta, cut into
    1 cm- (½ in-) wide strips
    (optional)

This incredibly easy soup is something I rustle up quickly when I need a quick lunch or starter. I love the aniseed flavours of tarragon. It is known in Italy as *dragoncello* – a wonderful name which conjures up images of medieval knights and mythical beasts. It may be so named as it is said to have been introduced to Siena by Charlemagne in 774, when it was used to make salsa verde (see page 123).

Heat half the oil in a large saucepan over a medium heat, then add the onions, a pinch of salt and pepper, and sauté until soft. Add the peas and 2 sprigs of the tarragon, and stir through. Pour in the stock and bring to the boil. Cook the peas for 5 minutes if frozen and 10 minutes if fresh.

Meanwhile, fry the pancetta (if using) in the remaining olive oil in a non-stick frying pan, until just crispy, then remove from the pan and set aside. When the peas are soft use a stick blender or food processor to blitz the soup until smooth. Serve scattered with the remaining tarragon, leaves stripped and roughly chopped, the pancetta, if using, and a swirl of good-quality olive oil.

swiss chard & egg soup

**SERVES
6 PEOPLE**

4 tablespoons extra-virgin
   olive oil
1 red onion, peeled and halved
   root to tip then finely sliced
   into half-moons
2 celery stalks, finely sliced
10 basil leaves
1 litre (34 fl oz/4¼ cups)
   warm Chicken or Vegetable
   Stock (see page 32 or 35),
   or hot water
3 heaped tablespoons
   tomato purée (paste)
1 kg (2 lb 3 oz) Swiss chard
   or spinach leaves, not
   including stalks, roughly
   chopped
1 teaspoon salt
¼ teaspoon dried chilli flakes
6 small slices thick crusty
   bread, toasted
1 garlic clove, peeled
6 eggs

Glorious, spicy, colourful *acquacotta* is from southern Tuscany in the Maremma area. There are myriad recipes that vary hugely from family to family, season to season and whether it was made in times of hardship when it was little more than its name suggests ('cooked water') or wealth when, as in this recipe, bread and eggs are added. Antonella Secciani's family is from Grosseto and she showed us the traditional way to make it in a terracotta pot with layers of bread, soup and beaten eggs. It is covered and wrapped in cloth so that the bread becomes soft and the residual warmth of the soup cooks the egg. This is our simple version, that we eat for breakfast, lunch and dinner. The quantity of leaves is abundant and should change according to the season, so feel free to swap the Swiss chard or spinach for kale or cabbage.

Heat the oil in a large saucepan with a lid over a low heat. Add the onion, celery, basil and a splash of the warm stock or water, and cook for around 15 minutes, until the onions and celery become soft and translucent. Stir the tomato purée into the remaining stock and pour into the pan, then add the chopped chard or spinach, salt and chilli flakes. Stir through until the spinach wilts and the soup bubbles. Reduce the heat, loosely cover the pan and leave to cook for 30–40 minutes until the soup is well combined. Taste and adjust the seasoning and chilli as necessary. Remove from the heat.

Ladle a layer of soup around 1 cm (½ in) thick into the bottom of a wide saucepan or casserole. Rub the toast slices with the clove of garlic lightly on one side and lay them into the pan garlic side up. Spoon the remaining soup over the bread and crack the eggs on top. Cover with a lid and cook over a medium heat until the eggs have just set. Remove from the heat and leave in a warm place for 5–10 minutes so that the bread can absorb the liquid from the soup. Serve in warm bowls with an egg for everyone.

tiziana's lentil soup

**SERVES
6 PEOPLE**

200 g (7 oz) small brown
  or green lentils
1–2 teaspoons salt
150 g (5 oz) Swiss chard with
  stalks, finely diced, or
  spinach leaves, finely
  shredded
1 long celery stalk, finely diced
2 tomatoes, fresh or tinned,
  finely diced
1 tablespoon best-quality
  extra-virgin olive
  oil, plus extra to serve
small handful of parsley,
  finely chopped
½–1 teaspoon dried chilli
  flakes, or to taste (optional)

We enjoyed this hearty soup at our cousin Tiziana's house. It was dressed with olive oil that was just three days old. The lentils were organic and grown just 1 km (0.6 miles) away and the Swiss chard was from her *orto*. This recipe is very easy and very pure – the flavours come from the lentils and fresh ingredients.

Soak the lentils for 15–20 minutes in a bowl of cold water. Drain and put them into a pan and fill with 1 litre (34 fl oz/4¼ cups) of fresh cold water, or until the lentils are just covered. Add 1 teaspoon of salt, bring to the boil, then reduce the heat and cook for 30 minutes.

While the lentils are cooking, put the Swiss chard, celery and tomatoes in a saucepan with a good pinch of salt, the oil, parsley and chilli (if using), and cover with a lid. Put over a low heat and let everything cook slowly for 15–20 minutes or until the vegetables have softened – it will form its own juice.

Drain the lentils and add them to the chard soup base, keeping the cooking water. Then add around 400 ml (13 fl oz/1¾ cups) of the lentil water (you don't want to add too much). Bring to the boil then reduce the heat to low and continue to cook for 45 minutes, covered. Add a little more cooking water if it looks dry. Season with salt to taste. Serve swirled with your best olive oil.

choux pastry with chicken livers, cream & lemon

**SERVES
6 PEOPLE**

1 quantity of choux pastry
(see page 74)
100 g (3½ oz) salted butter
2 tablespoons extra-virgin
olive oil
1 red onion, peeled and
finely chopped
2 garlic cloves, finely chopped
salt and freshly ground
black pepper
300 g (10½ oz) chicken livers
plain (all-purpose) flour,
for dusting
100 ml (3½ fl oz/scant ½ cup)
brandy or Vin Santo
250 ml (8½ fl oz/1 cup) hot
Chicken Stock (see page 32)
or water
small handful of parsley
leaves, roughly chopped
juice of 1 lemon
4 egg yolks
2 tablespoons double (heavy)
cream or whipping cream

This ancient traditional Tuscan recipe comes from the Middle Ages when gizzards, hearts and cock's combs were used up in this way. Catherine de' Medici was said to have loved this dish so much that she made herself ill eating too much of it. Normally it is not served in a choux bun, but we love this version, which was shown to us years ago by a Florentine chef visiting one of our restaurants. If you don't want to make the choux pastry, serve the *cibreo* with hot toast instead.

Make the pastry according to the instructions on page 74, but instead of making small mounds of the mixture on the baking tray, pipe it into 6 evenly-sized mounds spaced 6 cm (2½ in) apart and bake at 200°C (400°F/Gas 6) for 10 minutes, then turn the oven down to 170°C (340°F/Gas 3) for a further 15–17 minutes or until golden brown and firm inside. Remove from the oven and pierce a hole in the side of each bun. Leave to cool on a wire rack.

Heat half the butter and half the oil in a large frying pan. Add the onion and garlic with a good pinch of salt and plenty of black pepper, and sweat over a low heat for 10–15 minutes or until soft. Meanwhile, prepare the chicken livers by removing the tough connective tissue and cutting them into roughly 1 cm- (½ in-) wide strips. Dust the livers with flour and shake off the excess. Heat the remaining butter and oil in the pan containing the onion and garlic, season and fry until the chicken livers are browned all over. Pour in the brandy or Vin Santo and flambé to burn off the alcohol. If you prefer not to flambé, simply let the brandy bubble until the strong smell of alcohol disappears.

Add the stock or water and parsley and stir through, then cook over a medium heat for roughly 20 minutes or until the livers are cooked through and not pink inside.

Mix the lemon juice, egg yolks and cream together in a small bowl. Remove the pan from the heat and push the livers to one side of the pan so that the juices pool in one area. Pour the egg mixture into the juices and stir through quickly before mixing the sauce with the livers. Taste and adjust the seasoning as necessary.

Warm the choux buns. Split them open and lay one half of the bun down, ladle on some chicken livers and sauce, and top with the other half of the bun. Serve straight away.

grana padano timbale

SERVES
6 PEOPLE

unsalted butter, for greasing
2 eggs, beaten
125 ml (4 fl oz/½ cup)
     whole (full-fat) milk
125 ml (4 fl oz/½ cup) double
     (heavy) cream
good pinch of salt
good pinch of freshly ground
     black pepper
150 g (5 oz) finely grated
     Grana Padano

TO SERVE
2 ripe medium tomatoes,
     roughly chopped, to serve
small handful of basil leaves,
     to serve
good-quality extra-virgin
     olive oil, to serve

This is one of the best-selling dishes at our restaurant Caldesi in Campagna. The recipe was shown to us by Tuscan chef Riccardo Cappelli. It can be made in moulds and turned out, or cooked and served in small ramekins.

Preheat the oven to 160°C (320°F/Gas 3). Grease 6 × 150 ml (5 fl oz) dariole moulds or ramekins generously and put a circle of baking parchment at the bottom of each one. (You do not need to do this if you are not going to turn them out.)

Mix the beaten eggs with the milk, cream, salt and pepper. Add the grated cheese and stir it through. Pour the mixture into the moulds until they are three-quarters full then set them on a baking tray. Add enough water to the tray to come 2 cm (¾ in) up the sides of the moulds. Bake in the oven for 30 minutes or until golden brown on top and set. Serve with freshly chopped tomato, basil and a swirl of olive oil.

tuscan vegetable timbales in a pecorino cheese sauce

MAKES
8 × 100–150 ML (3½–5 FL OZ)
DARIOLE MOULDS OR RAMEKINS

FOR THE BÉCHAMEL
250 ml (8½ fl oz/1 cup)
    whole (full-fat) milk
30 g (1 oz) unsalted butter
1 small bay leaf
¼ teaspoon finely grated nutmeg
salt and freshly ground
    black pepper
2 tablespoons cornflour
    (cornstarch)

FOR THE SFORMATI
unsalted butter, for greasing
4 tablespoons sesame seeds
    (optional)
250–300 g (9–10½ oz) cooked
    spinach, squeezed dry
75 g (2½ oz) grated Parmesan
    or Grana Padano
3 egg whites, loosely whisked
salt and freshly ground
    black pepper
250–300 g (9–10½ oz) cooked
    and well-drained cauliflower
250–300 g (9–10½ oz) cooked
    and well-drained carrot

FOR THE CREAM SAUCE
100 ml (3½ fl oz/scant ½ cup)
    double (heavy) cream
75 g (2½ oz) grated Pecorino
    or Parmesan
freshly ground black pepper

TO SERVE
25 g (1 oz) pine nuts, toasted,
    to serve
freshly ground black pepper
good-quality extra-virgin
    olive oil
thyme leaves

Our good friend and fellow foodie Anna Hudson and I have had great fun playing with these little beauties, both with the flavours and layering up the colours. *Sformati* can be served as a *primo* with cheese sauce; with *secondi*; or for breakfast. We have given the recipe for making a layered *sformato* from carrot, cauliflower and spinach as that is our favourite. Most vegetables will work on their own if they have a strong flavour and are not too watery, such as courgette. *Sformati* are a great way to use up leftover vegetables, especially if they have been steamed *al cartoccio* (see page 237) as they have such an intense flavour. Our friend Antonella Secciani's way to make a cauliflower *sformato* is with sesame seeds in the mould; she serves it with a hearty stew like the *peposo* on page 208. The remaining egg yolks can be kept for making the custard on page 244 or the *fricassea* on page 106.

To make the béchamel, heat 200 ml (7 fl oz/¾ cup) of the milk in a medium saucepan with the butter, bay leaf, nutmeg, salt and pepper over a medium heat. Mix the cornflour into the remaining 50 ml (2 fl oz/¼ cup) of milk to make a smooth paste, then add this to the warm milk in the pan and stir well with a wooden spoon. Increase the heat and keep stirring until the sauce is thickened, then remove from the heat, discard the bay leaf and set aside.

To make the *sformati*, preheat the oven to 170°C (340°F/Gas 3). Grease the dariole moulds generously with butter and place a small circle of baking parchment at the bottom of each one. They can be dusted with sesame seeds at this point, if you wish.

Put the spinach, a third of the béchamel, a third of the cheese and 1 egg white into a food processor or use a bowl and stick blender. Add a good pinch of salt and a twist of black pepper. Blend until smooth and tip into a bowl. Do the same with the cauliflower and carrot mixtures, using up the remaining béchamel, cheese and eggs. Now divide the spinach mixture between the moulds, followed by the cauliflower mixture and lastly the carrot mixture, then set the moulds on a baking tray.

Add enough water to the tray to come 2 cm (¾ in) up the sides of the moulds. Bake in the oven for 30–35 minutes or until firm to the touch. Remove from the oven and leave to stand at room temperature for 5 minutes before turning out.

To make the cream sauce, heat the cream and cheese together in a small saucepan and serve with the *sformati*. Scatter the *sformati* with some toasted pine nuts, a twist of pepper, a drizzle of good-quality olive oil and a few thyme leaves.

pasta & gnocchi

Just over the border into Lazio is the small town of Cerveteri where there are a collection of Etruscan tombs. Far from a dry and dull museum, the Italians have turned these tombs into a piece of theatre as they immerse you in a recreation of Etruscan life. It is brilliant and well worth a visit. It is here that you can see a relief sculpture of what seems to be early pasta making. The carving shows figures mixing flour and water next to a rolling pin and a cutting machine. The Etruscans created *pici*, a hand-rolled pasta still massively popular today.

We watched Vincenzo Longhitano make *tortelli* (pasta parcels) in the Tuscan way as he has done for 40 years. He runs the tiny trattoria in Roccatederighi in the Grosseto area. He makes his pasta fresh every day for his customers as otherwise he feels it loses its flavour and texture. He seals the *tortelli* with a fork so that the grooves catch the *sugo* (sauce). Then he cuts *tagliatelle* (ribbons) with a knife to show it is made by hand and not by a machine. Finally, any off-cuts are made into *maltagliati* (misshapen pieces). Nothing is wasted.

Pasta and gnocchi are economical to make and actually not that difficult. Over the years, Giancarlo and I have taught hundreds of people to make them in our cookery school. If you have a small pasta machine you can make and cook pasta from start to finish in 30 minutes. Stuffed pasta takes a little longer, but in this chapter we show you how to make it.

As for the sauces, always have them hot and ready in a frying pan waiting for the pasta and not the other way around. If they are too dense, let them down with a little hot pasta water, or stock if you have it. Drain the pasta when it is just al dente (firm to the bite) and let it finish cooking in the sauce.

kale & ricotta gnocchi in sage & bacon butter

SERVES
6 AS A STARTER / 4 AS A MAIN
(MAKES APPROX. 36 GNOCCHI)

FOR THE GNOCCHI
300 g (10½ oz) fresh curly kale
    or cavolo nero, or 200 g
    (7 oz) cooked and thoroughly
    squeezed curly kale or
    cavolo nero leaves
250 g (9 oz/1 cup) ricotta,
    drained
100 g (3½ oz) grated Parmesan
    or Pecorino
1 egg
3 heaped tablespoons wheat or
    gluten-free flour, plus extra
    for dusting
¼ teaspoon finely grated
    nutmeg
1 teaspoon salt, plus extra
    for the cooking water
freshly ground black pepper
25 g (1 oz) grated Parmesan,
    plus extra, to serve

FOR THE BACON, BUTTER
AND SAGE SAUCE
100 g (3½ oz) unsalted butter
150 g (5 oz) unsmoked or
    smoked pancetta or bacon,
    cut into small strips
10 sage leaves
salt, to taste
freshly ground black pepper
    (optional)
30 g (1 oz) pine nuts, toasted
    (optional)

In Florence, the name of these gnocchi literally means 'nude' gnocchi as they are like the spinach and ricotta stuffing that you find in ravioli only without their pasta clothes. Some call them *strozzapreti*, meaning 'priest-stranglers', as apparently they were given to priests in the days of the *mezzadria* who were so greedy they almost choked on them (see pages 16–17). In Siena, they are known as *malfatti*, meaning 'badly made'. If you don't have kale, use 200 g (7 oz) of cooked and well-squeezed spinach or Swiss chard leaves instead. Serve them with the bacon, butter and sage sauce (omit the bacon for a vegetarian version), Memmo's Beef Ragù (see page 171) or the Homemade Tomato Sauce on page 40.

Start by making the gnocchi. If using fresh kale or cavolo nero, wash the leaves and pull away the tough stems. Roughly cut the leaves and boil them in salted water for 10 minutes. Drain well and set aside.

When cool enough to handle, thoroughly squeeze out the excess water from the kale (to the last drop!) and finely chop in a food processor (or by hand with a sharp knife on a board), then put into a bowl. Add the remaining ingredients for the gnocchi to the kale and stir through to combine. The mixture should be firm enough to handle and not wet and sticky. If it is too sticky, add a little more flour to the mix.

Roll the mixture into walnut-sized balls, making sure they are tightly packed so that they don't break up in the water. As you prepare the balls, put them on a floured surface. You can keep them like this in the fridge, loosely covered, for up to a day if you want to prepare them in advance.

Prepare the sauce by melting the butter in a large frying pan. Add the bacon, sage leaves, salt and pepper (if using) and fry until the bacon is cooked through and the sage leaves are lightly browned. Add a ladleful of hot water and stir well. Leave the sauce over a very low heat while you cook the gnocchi.

Bring a large pan of well salted water to the boil. Turn the heat down to medium – unlike when cooking pasta, you want a slow rolling boil, not a rapid boil. Drop the gnocchi carefully into the boiling water. Let the water come back up to the boil and cook for 3–4 minutes until the gnocchi rise up to the surface. Let them bob around for a further minute, then carefully remove them from the water with a slotted spoon and lower them gently into the butter sauce.

Fry them in the sauce for a few minutes until lightly browned. Stir the pine nuts into the sauce, if using. Serve with extra grated Parmesan on top.

chestnut & potato gnocchi

**SERVES
4 PEOPLE**

500 g (1 lb 2 oz) fluffy potatoes,
    such as Desiree or King
    Edward, unpeeled
75 g (2½ oz/scant ⅔ cup)
    chestnut or '00' flour
1 teaspoon fine salt, plus extra
    for the cooking water
freshly ground black pepper,
    to taste
1 egg, plus 1 egg yolk, beaten

Gnocchi are best made with potatoes that are neither too fluffy nor too smooth, and the Italians say they should be boiled in their skins so that the water doesn't saturate them. The secret to light gnocchi is to trap as much air inside as you can by pushing the cooked potatoes through a sieve, *passatutto* (food mill) or ricer. Freezing gnocchi before they are cooked can give an even better result than cooking from fresh, as they tend to hold their shape better. If you are not following a gluten-free diet, you can use '00' flour instead of chestnut flour if you prefer. Chestnut flour is naturally sweet and therefore the gnocchi lend themselves to a hearty meat ragù such as the one on page 171, or a simple sauce such as the butter and sage sauce on page 182.

Bring a large saucepan of salted water to the boil. Add the potatoes and cook them in their skins until tender – this may take up to 1 hour, depending on their size, but don't be tempted to cut them or they become watery. Remove the potatoes (don't drain away the cooking water) and peel them while they are still hot by holding a potato in one hand with a fork or a cloth and peeling away its skin with a knife in the other hand. Reserve the potato cooking water to cook the gnocchi.

Pass the potatoes through a sieve, ricer or food mill into a large bowl. Use a large metal spoon to fold in 50 g (2 oz/scant ½ cup) of the flour, the salt and pepper and the beaten eggs. Try to keep the movements light and brief to trap air in the mixture and form into a dough.

Scatter the remaining flour onto the work surface and use your hands to make long sausages from the dough around 2 cm (¾ in) wide. Cut the sausages into 2 cm (¾ in) lengths.

Bring the saucepan of reserved potato water to the boil, adding more hot water if necessary and a couple of teaspoons of salt. Drop in the gnocchi and cook for 2–4 minutes: when they bob up to the surface they are done. Drain well and toss into your chosen sauce, heated in a large frying pan.

If you plan to freeze your gnocchi before cooking, spread them out on a well-floured baking tray, making sure they don't touch each other, and put the tray in the freezer. When frozen, shake off any excess flour and transfer the gnocchi to a freezer bag to take up less space. Use within 3 months. To cook from frozen, allow an extra 1–2 minutes' cooking time.

fresh pasta

**MAKES ENOUGH PASTA FOR
6 AS A STARTER/4 AS A MAIN**

200 g (7 oz/1⅔ cups) '00' flour,
  plus a little extra if necessary
2 medium free-range eggs
  (preferably corn-fed,
  for colour)

This is the pasta recipe we always use and recommend (you can also find it in our *Sicily* book). It is: 1 egg to 100 g (3½ oz/scant 1 cup) '00' flour. Ideally, roll the pasta on a wooden surface, as the tiny particles of wood that project from the surface add texture, helping the pasta to absorb the sauce that will eventually coat it. Many Italians use a tablecloth for the same purpose. To save time, the pasta dough can be made in a food processor.

Pour the flour into a bowl and make a well in the centre. Crack the eggs into the well. Using a table knife, gradually mix the flour into the eggs. Keep mixing the eggs and flour together until they form a thick paste.

Use the fingertips of one hand to incorporate the rest of the flour and form a ball of dough. Discard the dry little crumbs. The dough should form a soft but firm, flexible ball. If it is still sticking to the palm of your hand, add a little more flour – but be careful to stop adding flour as soon as it stops sticking. If it's really dry and has many cracks, add a drop or two of water – do this in a bowl or the food processor.

Knead the pasta for 5–10 minutes, or until it springs back to the touch, the colour is uniform and, when cut open, the ball of dough is full of small air bubbles; this means you have kneaded it for long enough. Leave the pasta to rest for at least 20 minutes or up to 1 day, lightly dusted with flour and wrapped in cling film (plastic wrap) to prevent it from drying out while it rests.

long fresh pasta

SERVES
6 AS A STARTER / 4 AS A MAIN

1 batch of Fresh Pasta
(see page 167)
'00' flour, for dusting or coarse
semolina, to stop the pasta
sticking

Long ribbons of silky fresh pasta are commonplace in Tuscany as they are in most of northern Italy. Unique to Tuscany, however, is pappardelle, the extra-wide ribbons of fresh pasta made to go with a hearty beef ragù (see page 171) or the Kale & Sausage Pasta Sauce (see page 98). As fresh pasta is so absorbent it is better not served with watery sauces such as seafood; in this case dried pasta is the norm.

Follow the recipe for fresh pasta on page 167. After the resting time the pasta can be rolled out with a rolling pin or a pasta machine. To make any of the long pasta such as tagliatelle or pappardelle by hand, roll the pasta out into a rectangle using a heavy wooden rolling pin. Lightly dust the surface of the table, the pasta and the rolling pin with flour to prevent it sticking. If you use a pasta machine, flour the long strips on both sides. We tend to roll it out to a stop or two before the minimum (the finest setting on the machine), as in Tuscany ribbons of pasta such as pappardelle have a bite to them and are not as thin as in neighbouring Emilia Romagna.

As a general rule when the pasta is just transparent enough that you can see your fingers through it (about 1 mm thick) it is ready. Leave the pasta for 1–2 minutes to dry out in the air. Dust the work surface and the pasta with plenty of flour again to prevent it sticking to itself. Gently fold over one short edge, making a flap of about 3 cm (1¼ in). Now do the same with the other short edge. Fold the edges over again and again, sprinkling flour over the surface to stop the dough sticking to itself. Stop when the folded edges meet in the middle. Cut across the folds into the desired thicknesses to make the *pasta lunga*, the thinnest being tagliolini and the fattest pappardelle (2–3 cm/¾–1¼ in) wide. Slide a long knife underneath the centre, matching the blunt edge of the knife to where the two folded edges come together. Hold and twist the knife in the air and the pasta ribbons will fall down in cut lengths either side.

When cut, pull out into individual strands and toss with coarse semolina or a little more flour. Don't pile the pasta high but leave it in a single layer or the weight will cause it to stick together. Cook within the hour. The cooking time should be 2–3 minutes, or until *al dente*, in a pan of boiling salted water.

gluten-free fresh pasta

SERVES
6 AS A STARTER / 4 AS A MAIN

50 g (2 oz/generous ¼ cup) gluten-free plain (all-purpose) flour

50 g (2 oz/generous ⅓ cup) buckwheat flour

175 g (6 oz/scant 1½ cups) tapioca flour (tapioca starch)

1 heaped tablespoon xantham gum

180 g (6¼ oz) egg (approx. 3 large eggs)

1 tablespoon extra-virgin olive oil

2–3 tablespoons cold water

This recipe was first printed in our *Sicily* book as in recent years we have discovered that Giancarlo and our son Giorgio cannot tolerate wheat in their diets. This recipe was a saving grace for us. It can be used for cut ribbons as well as stuffed and shaped pasta.

Put all the ingredients, including 2 tablespoons of the cold water, into a food processor and blend until a ball of dough forms. If it is very dry and doesn't form a ball, add another tablespoon of water. You are aiming for a firm but pliable dough. Knead the dough for a few minutes to ensure it is well blended. Wrap in cling film (plastic wrap) and rest for 30 minutes at room temperature, or if you prefer to keep it longer it can be left up to 1 day in the fridge.

If you don't have a food processor, tip the dry ingredients into a bowl and stir to combine. Make a well in the centre of the ingredients and add the eggs with the oil and 2 tablespoons of water. Use a table knife to break up the eggs and combine the dry ingredients little by little. Eventually your knife will become ineffective, so use your hands to bring the dough together into a ball. If it is very dry and hard add 1 tablespoon more water. Knead and rest the dough as above.

After the dough has rested, use as fresh pasta, rolling the dough by hand or through a machine, remembering to use gluten-free flour for dusting.

memmo's beef ragù

SERVES
16–20 PEOPLE

FOR THE SOFFRITTO
200 g (7 oz) carrots
200 g (7 oz) celery stalks
200 g (7 oz) red or white onions,
    peeled
3 garlic cloves, peeled
2 sprigs of rosemary
100 ml (3½ fl oz/scant ½ cup)
    extra-virgin olive oil
salt and freshly ground
    black pepper

FOR THE RAGÚ
2 kg (4 lb 6 oz) beef,
    coarsely minced (ground)
500 ml (17 fl oz/2¼ cups)
    red wine
1.2 kg (2 lb 10 oz) tinned
    plum tomatoes

Tuscan meat ragù is rich and herby in flavour compared to its neighbouring Bolognese ragù, which usually contains no herbs or garlic. We always make a lot of this when we cook it as it freezes well. Giancarlo's father, Memmo, used to make it every 14 days, and he would pour it into glass jars and store it in the fridge. Every day at 1 pm he would unscrew a jar and warm it up to have with his pasta. For two weeks he had an easy lunch before he made the next batch. We ask our local butcher to give us a fatty cut of beef, around 15 per cent fat, and coarsely grind the meat for us. Giancarlo's family ate this ragù with fresh fettucine or dried pasta such as spaghetti, but it is also lovely on soft cheesy polenta (see page 37) or roasted vegetables (see page 230).

In a large frying pan (skillet), make a *soffritto* with the carrots, celery, onions, garlic, rosemary, oil and seasoning, by following the instructions on page 28, but finely chop the garlic with the other vegetables. When the *soffritto* is soft, remove the rosemary sprigs.

To make the ragù, add the mince to the *soffritto* and stir well. Cook the for around 20 minutes, stirring frequently and allowing the water to evaporate from the pan. Add the wine and let it reduce until the smell of alcohol dissipates. Pour the tomatoes into a bowl and crush them with your hands (this is Giancarlo's way; my way is to use a potato masher when they are in the pan – the choice is yours!). Add the tomatoes to the pan, stir and bring to the boil. Turn down the heat and continue to cook for around 2 hours, uncovered, over a low heat. If the heat is low, it shouldn't catch, but do keep an eye on it and add a little hot water if it looks dry. Taste and adjust the seasoning.

Use straight away or allow to cool and store in the fridge in a covered container for 1 week, or freeze for up to 3 months.

ravioli filled with tomato & bread stuffing in a warm mozzarella cream

SERVES
6 AS A STARTER (MAKES 24 RAVIOLI MEASURING APPROX. 6 CM/2½ IN WIDE)

FOR THE FILLING
50 g (2 oz) stale country-style bread
150 ml (5 fl oz/⅔ cup) Homemade Tomato Sauce (see page 40)
10 g (½ oz) basil leaves, roughly chopped

FOR THE RAVIOLI
1 quantity of Fresh Pasta (see page 167)
coarse semolina or '00' flour, for dusting

FOR THE MOZZARELLA CREAM
1 × 125 g (4 oz) ball of mozzarella, roughly chopped, plus the water/brine from the bag
125 ml (4 fl oz/½ cup) double (heavy) cream
125 g (4 oz) unsalted butter
salt, to taste

TO SERVE
25 g (1 oz) salted or unsalted butter, cubed
extra-virgin olive oil, for drizzling
25 g (1 oz) grated Parmesan
freshly ground black pepper

This is one of Daniele Sera's signature dishes that he makes at the stunning hotel Castello di Casole in central Tuscany. He has taken a typical Tuscan recipe for a tomato, basil and bread soup called *pappa al pomodoro* (see page 141) and made it into a filling for fresh pasta. These tangy, tomatoey parcels are served in a warm bath of melted mozzarella and cream: dairy heaven in a sauce. (You can enjoy it as it is or make it thicker with cornflour/cornstarch blended with a little of the sauce.) The result is sublime.

To make the filling, soak the bread in a small bowl of cold water until soaked through. Remove the bread from the bowl and squeeze out the water. Put the tomato sauce in a saucepan over a medium heat and add the bread to it – it will melt into the pan. Add the basil and stir through. Leave to cook over a low heat for 15 minutes or until the bread has broken down and thickened the sauce. Remove from the heat, transfer to a bowl and allow to cool to room temperature.

To make the ravioli, take half the fresh pasta. Flour the work surface but don't flour the top side of the pasta or it will be hard to seal. Roll out the pasta using a rolling pin or a pasta machine until you can see your hand through it. If using a pasta machine set it on the second to last setting – the very last setting makes the thinnest pasta but this is too fragile for ravioli – and roll out 2 equally sized sheets of pasta.

Dot heaped teaspoons of the filling at even intervals (two fingers' width apart is ideal) onto one of the sheets and place another sheet of the same length over the top. Press down around the filling to expel the air and seal the pasta sheets together. Using a pasta wheel or a sharp knife, cut the ravioli into even 5 cm (2 in) squares. Set the shapes aside on a surface dusted with flour or semolina (semolina is good as it doesn't stick to the pasta). Repeat with the remaining pasta until the filling is used up.

For the mozzarella cream, put the mozzarella, the brine from the bag, the cream and butter into a saucepan and set over a high heat to melt. When the cheese has melted pass it through a sieve to remove any remaining small lumps of cheese. Taste and add salt as necessary.

To serve, warm the mozzarella cream sauce over a gentle heat. Drop the pasta into well-salted boiling water and cook for just 2–3 minutes. Drain and put into a warm dish with the butter and toss the bowl to combine – this will stop the pasta sticking. Put a ladleful of mozzarella cream into each bowl and place the pasta on top. Drizzle some olive oil on top of each dish, sprinkle over a little grated Parmesan, season with black pepper and serve straight away.

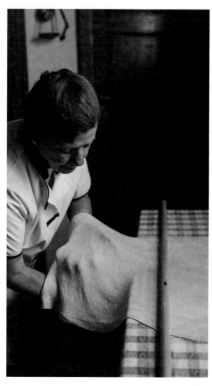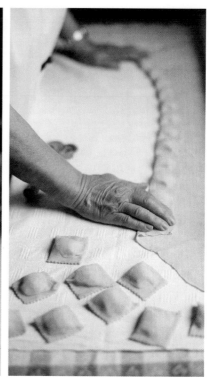

RAVIOLI DI MUGELLO

ravioli stuffed with potato & cheese

MAKES
200 G (7 OZ) FILLING FOR
36–40 (4 CM/1½ IN SQUARE)
RAVIOLI

FOR THE FILLING
200 g (7 oz) fluffy potatoes
    such as King Edward
    or Desiree, unpeeled
1 small garlic clove, peeled
5 g (¼ oz) parsley
generous pinch of finely
    grated nutmeg
½ teaspoon salt
35 g (1¼ oz) grated Parmesan
freshly ground black pepper

FOR THE RAVIOLI
1 quantity of Fresh Pasta
    (see page 167)
coarse semolina or '00' flour,
    for dusting

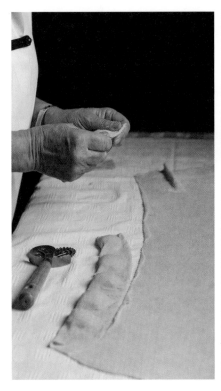

Mugello is a small town in the north of Tuscany and their recipe for these soft pillows of pasta filled with potato and cheese has become famous. Any leftover stuffing can be made into small patties and fried in oil. These are ideal to serve with a ragù such as the Duck Ragù on page 177 or Memmo's Beef Ragù on page 171.

To make the filling, bring a large pan of salted water to the boil, add the potatoes and cook them in their skins until tender. It will take up to 1 hour for large ones, but don't be tempted to cut them up or they become watery. Traditionally, they are always boiled, but they are also good pierced with a fork a few times and baked or cooked in a microwave. Meanwhile, finely cut the garlic and parsley together on a board. When the potatoes are cooked through, drain and peel them while they are still hot by holding a potato in one hand with a cloth or a fork and peeling or scraping away its skin with a knife. Ideally, pass the potatoes through a ricer, sieve or food mill into a bowl (if you don't have any of those, use a masher). Mix in the garlic, parsley, nutmeg, Parmesan, salt

and a good twist of pepper. Taste and adjust the seasoning as necessary. The filling should have a fairly strong flavour as it needs to be detectable through the pasta and sauce.

To make the ravioli, follow the instructions for the ravioli on page 173. Serve tossed in a pan with warm Duck Ragù (see page 177) or Memmo's Beef Ragù (see page 171).

duck ragù

SERVES
6 PEOPLE

5 tablespoons extra-virgin
   olive oil
4 large duck legs (about
   1.5 kg/3 lb 5 oz)
salt and freshly ground
   black pepper
2 medium red onions,
   peeled and finely chopped
2 medium carrots,
   finely chopped
1 small celery stalk,
   finely chopped
4 bay leaves
200 g (7 oz) Fresh Tomato
   Passata (see page 41),
   or tinned tomatoes
300 ml (10 fl oz/1¼ cups)
   red wine
400–700 ml (13–24 fl oz/
   1¾–3 cups) chicken, meat
   or vegetable stock (see
   pages 32–35), or hot water

TO SERVE
fresh pasta of choice
   (see pages 167–69)
Ravioli stuffed with Potato
   & Cheese (see page 174)

Nana is Tuscan for 'duck', hence the Italian name for the sauce. Historically, many families in Tuscany who had a garden would have had ducks, therefore it was simple to cook one for lunch. Ducks are roasted, cooked in sauce or, in this case, used to make the famous Tuscan duck ragù. We use legs because they are cheaper than the breasts and have more flavour. You can use the whole duck, jointed, but since you have to pick the meat from the bones it is easier to do this with the legs. This type of sauce is typically served with fresh pasta such as tagliatelle or maltagliati – the misshapen pieces – or the potato-filled *Ravioli di Mugello* (see page 174), and is not normally served with cheese.

Heat the oil in a large non-stick frying pan over a high heat until hot, then lay the duck legs skin side down in the pan. Season generously. Leave to brown for about 10 minutes or until the skin is golden and crisp, then turn them over to brown on the other side. Now, season this side of the legs. Reduce the heat to medium and add the chopped onions, carrots, celery and the bay leaves. Stir through then tuck the bay leaves under the duck. Cook for around 10 minutes, stirring occasionally.

Meanwhile blend the tinned tomatoes (if using instead of passata) in a food processor or push them through a sieve into a bowl. Add the wine to the duck pan and allow it to bubble and evaporate for a few minutes, and for the strong smell of alcohol to diminish, then add the tomatoes and 400 ml (13 fl oz/ 1¾ cups) of the stock or water. Bring to the boil, remove the bay leaves and taste the sauce. Add seasoning to taste and loosely cover the pan with a lid. Leave to cook over a low heat for around 1 hour or until the meat falls off the bones easily (push a knife into the meat to see how soft it is). You may need to add the remaining stock if it looks a little dry. Remove the pan from the heat and leave to cool.

When the legs are cool enough to touch, remove them from the pan and pull off the meat and skin. Discard the bones and skin. Roughly chop the meat with a large knife, then put it back into the pan and stir through. If eating straight away, heat through and mix with cooked and drained pasta in the pan and serve. Otherwise, chill and keep in the fridge for up to 4 days, or freeze for up to 3 months.

PICI WITH
ANCHOVY
BREADCRUMBS
(PAGE 181)

wood pigeon ragù

**SERVES
8 PEOPLE**

FOR THE PIGEON
4 pigeons, approx. 175 g (6 oz)
    each, quartered (with the
    giblets left in)
2 teaspoons salt
½ teaspoon freshly ground
    black pepper
120 ml (4 fl oz/½ cup)
    extra-virgin olive oil
3 slices of rigatino or
    unsmoked bacon,
    roughly chopped
500 ml (17 fl oz/2¼ cups)
    Beef Bone Broth (see
    page 34)
Fabrizio's Hand-Rolled Pasta
    Strands (see opposite),
    to serve (optional)

FOR THE MARINADE
½ red onion, peeled and
    roughly sliced into wedges
small handful of parsley
handful of sage leaves
2 bay leaves
5 sprigs of rosemary
15 juniper berries
fresh red chilli, to taste
2 celery stalks
1 carrot
750 ml (25 fl oz/3 cups)
    red wine

FOR THE BATTUTO
small handful of sage leaves
2 sprigs of rosemary,
    leaves picked
1 fat garlic clove

Fabrizio Biagi was a hunter and made *pici*, the hand-rolled pasta, to go with ragù made from his catch (see recipe opposite). Now his time is taken up cooking and painting so he leaves the hunting to other men.

Fabrizio showed me the juniper berries that he collected in the woods nearby. Apparently they are harvested in an upturned umbrella – the locals bang the branches and the berries fall into it. Antonella took me to the window and pointed out where the pigeons came from on a nearby farm as well as the olive trees that provided the cooking oil. Between them they could point out the provenance of nearly everything we were about to eat.

The ragù, also known as *ragù dell'aia* (meaning what was roaming around the farmyard earlier!), works for other birds such as pheasant, quails or partridge, as well as other types of pasta. My favourite is fresh pappardelle or, if using dried pasta, spaghetti would work well. Fabrizio feels that the time, wine and *aroma* (flavourings) used for marinating are the most important part as the flavour is developed then. He likes to use a local Chianti wine.

Wash the pigeons in cold water to get rid of the blood, then dry them with a clean towel. Put them in a large bowl with all the marinade ingredients and leave them to marinate in the fridge for 1–2 hours.

Meanwhile, make the *battuto* by using a mezzaluna or a sharp knife to finely chop the ingredients together. After the birds have marinated, drain them, keeping the marinade and fishing out the vegetables. Put the pigeons onto paper towel to dry it out or, as Fabrizio kept saying, *scollare bene* (pat dry with the towel). Season them with the salt and pepper.

Put the oil in a large pan over a medium heat and, when hot, sauté the birds with the *battuto*. Brown them all over for about 10 minutes. Wash the vegetables from the marinade briefly in cold water, cut them into small pieces, then add them to the pan with the rigatino or bacon. Fry for 10–15 minutes or until soft. Add 200 ml (7 fl oz/generous ¾ cup) of the marinade. Cook over a medium heat until the scent of wine has disappeared and the sauce has reduced. Pour in the stock to almost cover the meat. Bring to the boil and cover the pan. Reduce the heat and simmer for 1–1½ hours or until the meat falls from the bones. Remove from the heat and leave until the pigeon is cool enough to touch. Pick the meat and skin from the bones, taking care to remove and discard any small bones. Chop the meat finely on a board with a large cook's knife or mezzaluna. Put this chopped mixture back into the pan and reheat to further reduce the sauce. If it looks dry, add a little hot water.

Meanwhile, if using, cook the *pici* (see below) in plenty of salted boiling water with a dash of oil until al dente. They will take 7–10 minutes, depending on their size. Drain and toss into the pan to combine with the sauce. Serve in warm bowls straight away.

fabrizio's hand-rolled pasta strands

**SERVES
8 PEOPLE**

1 kg (2 lb 3 oz/8 cups) '00' flour
3 g (⅕ oz) salt
1 tablespoon oil
500 ml (17 fl oz/2 cups)
    cold water

Fabrizio and his wife Antonella and daughter Ilaria invited us to their house to help them make ragù (see recipe opposite) and *pici*. We spent an incredible morning together making stock, drinking coffee, eating wet walnuts and chatting while the pigeons cooked in the pot. The family squabbled happily about who rolled the best *pici*, and after a hectic few days I felt myself finally slow down to the Tuscan pace of life. We had spent almost the whole day on one dish but what a joy it was. Not just lunch, but an invitation to partake in the skills of the Tuscan kitchen; a wonderful way to spend the day.

Put the flour in a large bowl and add the salt and oil. Add a little cold water, a splash at a time (you may not need all of it), and mix it into the flour with a wooden spoon. When the dough starts to come together and the spoon is rendered useless, put the dough onto a large wooden board and knead it with your hands. Put the crumbs into a bowl and add a splash more water. Bring that amount into a dough with your hands and then mix the two together. Add a little more flour as necessary and knead for a good 10 minutes until the ball is smooth. Wrap in cling film (plastic wrap) and leave to rest for 30 minutes. (In summer I put it in the fridge but you can leave it out in winter.)

Keep the bulk of the dough wrapped in cling film so that it doesn't dry out. Cut a palm-sized piece off and put it onto the table, then roll it out with a rolling pin to a thickness of 3 mm (⅛ in). They should be like thick lengths of spaghetti. Use a pizza cutter to cut the piece into 5 mm- (¼ in-) wide strips. Use your hands to roll the strips into long strands, stretching them as you roll by spreading your fingers out. Leave them separated from one another on a floured board. They can rest here for a few hours or overnight before cooking. To cook, bring a pan of salted water to the boil and cook for 8–10 minutes.

●

Variation: *Pici* with anchovy breadcrumbs
Fry 200 g (7 oz/generous 2 cups) coarse breadcrumbs from a stale loaf with 10 salted anchovy fillets, 4 finely chopped cloves of garlic and 1 teaspoon chilli flakes in 8 tablespoons of olive oil for around 5 minutes, or until crunchy. Toss with the *pici* and add grated Parmesan to taste.

●

CAPPELLI DI FRATE

large ravioli filled with spinach & an egg yolk

SERVES
6 PEOPLE

FOR THE FILLING
200 g (7 oz) spinach, cooked
   and squeezed dry
30 g (1 oz / ⅛ cup) fresh ricotta
30 g (1 oz) grated Parmesan,
   plus extra to serve
¼ teaspoon freshly grated
   nutmeg
¼ teaspoon salt
freshly ground black pepper,
   to taste
6 egg yolks or 6 quail's eggs
25 g (1 oz) grated Parmesan,
   to serve

FOR THE RAVIOLI
1 quantity Fresh Pasta (see
   page 167)
coarse semolina or '00' flour,
   for dusting

FOR THE SAUCE
150 g (5 oz) salted butter
18–20 sage leaves
salt and freshly ground
   black pepper
30 g (1 oz) pine nuts, toasted

These large filled ravioli (*cappelli di frate*), named after the shape of a monk's hat, make a stunning dinner party dish as the egg yolk oozes out as you eat them. Do practise before you make them for friends however, as you have to learn to be gentle with them in the cooking and serving. We use an 11 cm (4¼ in) pastry cutter but you could instead draw a knife around a small 10–12 cm (4–5 in) diameter saucer to make the circles of pasta. Use the leftover egg whites to make Marietta's Pannacotta on page 253.

Start by making the filling. Finely chop the cooked spinach on a chopping board or in a food processor. Put it into a bowl with the ricotta, Parmesan, nutmeg, salt and pepper, and mix together thoroughly. Taste and adjust the seasoning as necessary. Cover and set aside until required.

Roll out half the pasta at a time, following the instructions on page 173 to the width of the pasta machine. Lay the first sheet onto a floured board and cut the length in half. Don't get flour onto the pasta on the top side. Use an 11 cm (4¼ in) cutter to lightly make 3 circles – these will be the size of your finished *cappelli del frate*. Use a spoon to place 3 equal heaps of half of the filling into the circles. Lightly press the filling outwards leaving a 1 cm (½ in) border around

each mound with a well in each one large enough for the yolk. Put 1 egg yolk or 1 quail's egg into each well. Lay the other length of pasta on top and press down, pushing out the air and sealing the edges down. You shouldn't need water to stick the pasta together if there is no flour between the edges that are stuck down, but if it is dry, brush lightly with water to help it stick. Use your cutter to cut through the layers of pasta right through to the board. Set aside on a floured plate and make up the rest. Leave on a floured plate for no longer than 2 hours in the fridge.

To cook, bring a large pan of salted water to a rolling boil. Meanwhile, make the sauce by melting the butter in a large frying pan. Add the sage leaves, a pinch of salt, a few twists

of pepper and toasted pine nuts and fry for a couple of minutes. Add a ladleful of pasta cooking water and stir well. Keep the sauce warm but not bubbling while you cook the pasta.

Gently lower the ravioli into the boiling water, and stir gently to make sure they don't stick to one another. Cook for 4 minutes for a soft yolk and 6 minutes for firm. When cooked, remove the ravioli gently with a slotted spoon and put them into the warm butter and sage sauce. Shake the pan to coat the pasta and serve immediately in warm bowls with the sauce and grated Parmesan.

secondi

Secondi, the 'second course', is usually a form of protein in an Italian meal and follows a starter, or *primo*, of a soup or pasta. Inland Tuscany *secondi* is likely to be meat, with fish more popular on the coast. We love to tour Tuscan markets and collect ideas from the stalls. The butchers are the most interesting to me as it seems they just can't leave a piece of meat alone. Neatly tied packages of stuffed tenderloins, turkey rolls filled with cheese, joints ready for the oven tied with rosemary, and rolled and filled rabbit are crammed into chilled cabinets. There are vegetarian offerings like spinach patties and stuffed vegetables available too, showing the rising trend in non-meat-eaters. We have chosen a range of *secondi* for this chapter, from the ancient *peposo* (see page 208) to personal favourites such as the Rabbit in White Wine (see page 199), and our own invention of the porcini loaf (see page 205), inspired by those market stalls.

florentine pancakes

**SERVES
6 (MAKES 10–12 PANCAKES)**

FOR THE PANCAKE BATTER
1 egg
½ teaspoon salt
150 g (5 oz/scant 1¼ cups)
    buckwheat flour
550–600 ml (18½–20 fl oz/
    2⅓–2½ cups) milk
extra-virgin olive oil or lard,
    for frying

FOR THE FILLING
250 g (9 oz) cooked, squeezed
    and finely chopped spinach
250 g (9 oz) ricotta
25 g (1 oz) grated Parmesan
¼ teaspoon finely
    grated nutmeg
salt and freshly ground
    black pepper

TO SERVE
400 g (14 oz) Homemade
    Tomato Sauce (see page 40)
    or Fresh Tomato Passata
    (see page 41)
500 g (1 lb 2 oz) Béchamel
    Sauce (see page 189)
25 g (1 oz) grated Parmesan

An Italian lady showed me a brilliant trick for frying pancakes: cut a small potato in half and spear the rounded side with a fork. Dip the flat side into oil in a small bowl and use it to wipe a thin layer of oil around the frying pan – it doesn't absorb the oil like a piece of paper towel. You can use a tin of Italian plum tomatoes as the passata – just purée them with a stick blender or in a food processor. The pancakes can be made with any flour, but do adjust the milk quantity accordingly to reach the same consistency. The batter is easier to work with if it is made at least 30 minutes in advance. It can be made a day in advance and kept in the fridge covered in cling film (plastic wrap). Traditionally, fine white '00' flour is used for the pancakes but we like to use nutty-flavoured buckwheat, which, despite its name, has no connection to wheat. It is related to the rhubarb family, is very nutritious and contains no gluten. This recipe makes slightly more pancakes than you need, to allow for a few mishaps!

To make the pancake batter, whisk the egg, salt and flour together in a large bowl, then gradually add the milk, whisking constantly, until you have a very smooth batter the consistency of single cream. Let it stand at room temperature for at least 30 minutes (or longer in the fridge – overnight is fine).

Meanwhile, make the filling by mixing the ingredients together in a bowl and adding seasoning to taste.

While you fry the pancakes, leave a whisk in the bowl, as you need to stir the mixture thoroughly each time you add some batter to the pan. Wipe a little oil in a 25 cm (10 in) non-stick frying pan using a halved potato on a fork or a piece of paper towel (see intro). Pour in 75 ml (2½ fl oz/⅓ cup) of batter with a ladle or small measuring jug, swirling it around the pan to coat the base evenly. Fry the pancake over a medium–high heat for 2–3 minutes, flipping it over when one side is lightly browned to cook the other. Transfer it to a plate. Fry the rest of the batter in the same way, stacking the pancakes on the plate as you make them. While you are frying the pancakes, preheat the oven to 180°C (350°F/Gas 4).

To serve, spoon half of the tomato sauce or passata and half of the béchamel onto the base of an ovenproof dish (approximately 35 × 20 × 5 cm/ 14 × 8 × 2 in). Spread each pancake with 3 heaped tablespoons of the ricotta and spinach filling, covering half the pancake then rolling it up. Lay the pancakes in the dish. Top with the remaining tomato sauce or passata, followed by the béchamel. Scatter over the Parmesan and bake for about 30 minutes, or until the cheese has started to brown on top.

béchamel sauce

MAKES
350 ML (12 FL OZ/1½ CUPS)

350 ml (12 fl oz/1½ cups)
    whole (full-fat) milk
1 small onion, peeled
    and halved
1 bay leaf
good pinch each of finely
    grated nutmeg, salt and
    freshly ground black pepper
35 g (1¼ oz) salted butter
25 g (1 oz) plain (all-purpose)
    flour or cornflour
    (cornstarch)

Besciamella was originally a Tuscan sauce. The recipe was taken to France with Catherine de' Medici's chef in the 1500s. This is Giancarlo's version. He uses more butter than flour, which means it blends in easily and there are no lumps.

Put the milk, onion halves, bay leaf, nutmeg, salt and black pepper in a medium saucepan over a medium heat and bring to a gentle boil.

Meanwhile, make a roux: melt the butter in a small saucepan and stir in the flour. Cook the butter and flour for a few minutes over a medium heat, stirring constantly. Remove the bay leaf and onion from the milk, then add the roux to the milk, whisking furiously. Cook for 2–3 minutes or until the sauce thickens. Adjust the seasoning to taste and remove from the heat. Cover the surface of the béchel with cling film (plastic wrap) or a circle of dampened baking parchment to stop a skin forming until you are ready to use it.

●

Tip: If, when you come to use the béchamel, you find it too thick, add a little milk to thin it out. Reheating it also helps loosen it.

●

stuffed vegetables

SERVES
4–6 PEOPLE

8 large portobello mushrooms or 4 red (bell) peppers, halved, cored and seeds removed

FOR THE SOFFRITTO
1 small carrot, finely chopped
1 red onion, peeled and finely chopped
1 celery stalk and a few leaves, finely chopped
small handful of parsley, finely chopped
4 tablespoons extra-virgin olive oil
salt and freshly ground black pepper

FOR THE FILLING
5 tablespoons extra-virgin olive oil
1 garlic clove, peeled and lightly crushed
salt and freshly ground black pepper
500 g (1 lb 2 oz) minced (ground) meat (such as pork, beef, turkey or chicken)
25 g (1 oz) grated Parmesan or Pecorino
1 egg

Elena Rosini lives in a little second-floor flat in an old building in the heart of Siena. She works every day and likes to cook good, simple food for her and her partner. You can see the care she takes and that she cooks with love as she constantly tastes and adjusts the recipe.

We visited Elena in summer and she showed us how to stuff and cook round courgettes (zucchini) and large tomatoes. However, she told us that throughout the year, from the first courgettes to summer aubergines (eggplants), autumn mushrooms and winter pumpkins (squash), there will be a way to stuff them. You can serve them at room temperature or hot, for summer or winter accordingly and, once cold, they reheat really well for a quick meal. Cooking them partially under foil stops them drying out and intensifies the flavour.

Preheat the oven to 180°C (350°F/Gas 4). Make the *soffritto* using the carrot, onion, celery and parsley together with the oil and some salt and pepper for 10–15 minutes over a low heat until soft (see page 28). If using mushrooms, finely chop the stalks and add to the *soffritto*.

To make the filling, heat the oil with the garlic and add a pinch of salt and pepper. Remove the *soffritto* from the heat and put it into a bowl with the minced meat, cheese, egg and a little more seasoning. Stir to combine.

Fill the mushroom or peppers with the filling mixture and lay them in an ovenproof dish. (Any leftover mixture can be made into patties and cooked alongside the vegetables). Drizzle over the remaining olive oil and pour in 100 ml (3½ fl oz/scant ½ cup) water around the vegetables. Cover the dish with foil and bake in the oven for 30 minutes. Remove the foil and continue to cook for around 15 minutes or until the meat is golden brown and the vegetables are cooked through. Serve with sautéed greens or any of the salads on pages 87–91.

slow-cooked squid with spinach & chilli

**SERVES
6 PEOPLE**

6 tablespoons extra-virgin
   olive oil, plus extra to serve
1 white onion, peeled and
   finely chopped
2 garlic cloves, peeled
   and lightly crushed,
   plus 1 garlic clove, peeled,
   to serve
½–1 fresh red chilli, finely
   chopped, to taste, or
   ½ teaspoon dried chilli
   flakes or chilli oil
salt and freshly ground
   black pepper
500 g (1 lb 2 oz) cleaned squid,
   body cut into 1 cm (½ in)
   rings and tentacles and
   wings roughly chopped
250 ml (8½ fl oz/1 cup) dry
   white wine
800 g (1 lb 12 oz) tinned whole
   plum tomatoes
300 g (10½ oz) Swiss chard
   or spinach, tough stalks
   removed and leaves roughly
   chopped
200ml (7 fl oz/generous ¾ cup)
   hot water
1 crusty loaf, sliced
   and toasted, to serve

We first ate this dish in Livorno in a small trattoria around 18 years ago and I still remember it now. It was a cold day and the heat of the dish combined with the chilli and meltingly soft calamari was so welcome. It can be made with Swiss chard or spinach leaves and is a good dish to make in advance. It keeps well for around 3 days in the fridge and reheats quickly when needed. Other types of fish can be made *in zimino*, meaning cooked with tomatoes or green leaves, a term that dates back to the 12th century. This recipe was popular in 17th-century Florence and is found today in plenty of Tuscan restaurants.

Heat the oil in a large wide saucepan over a low heat. Add the onion, garlic, chilli, season with salt and pepper, and cook for 5–7 minutes, or until the onions are soft and tender. Add the squid to the pan, increase the heat to medium and cook for about 10 minutes until the squid rings are white, stirring frequently. Pour in the wine and bring to the boil. Reduce the heat to low and allow the alcohol to evaporate for 5–7 minutes. Put the tomatoes into a bowl and break them up with your hands or a potato masher so that they form a soft, pulpy sauce. Add the leaves, tomatoes and water to the pan, and bring to the boil. Reduce the heat to simmer and continue to cook for 1–1½ hours, or until the squid is really tender and soft. Season to taste.

Serve with toasted crusty bread rubbed with garlic and dressed with a little of your best olive oil.

swordfish alla livornese

**SERVES
4 PEOPLE**

400 g (14 oz) potatoes, peeled
    and cut into approx. 2 cm
    (¾ in) dice (optional)
2 garlic cloves, peeled
10 g (½ oz) parsley, hard stems
    removed, plus a little extra,
    roughly chopped, to serve
fresh red chilli, to taste,
    or ¼ teaspoon dried
    chilli flakes
salt, to taste
5 tablespoons extra-virgin
    olive oil
250 g (9 oz) Homemade Tomato
    Sauce (see page 40) or
    Fresh Tomato Passata
    (see page 41)
200 ml (7 fl oz/generous
    ¾ cup) warm water
1 tablespoon capers, rinsed
small handful of black olives
    (stones in)
freshly ground black pepper
approx. 4 swordfish steaks
    around 2 cm (¾ in) thick
    (about 125 g/4 oz per steak)
'00' or plain (all-purpose) flour,
    for dredging

Livorno is a port on the west coast of Tuscany. It might not be an obvious destination while holidaying in Tuscany but it has a fabulous, huge market not only for fish but everything else you could imagine. We love going there to sample and buy all sorts of ingredients to bring home. We often seem to be the only tourists and I love to watch all the locals buying their fresh seafood. Cooking fish *alla Livornese* means to fry the fish first, then serve it with a tomato and garlic sauce. The potatoes are optional but do help to fill up our hungry teenage boys.

If you're serving the fish with potatoes, put them in a pan of salted water, bring to the boil, and cook until just tender. Drain and set aside.

Make a *battuto* by finely chopping together one of the garlic cloves with the 10 g (½ oz) parsley, the chilli and a good pinch of salt (see page 29). Heat 2 tablespoons of the oil in a large non-stick frying pan over a medium heat and add the *battuto*. Fry for 2–3 minutes. Add the tomato sauce or passata and water and bring to the boil. Reduce the heat and cook for 10 minutes. Add the capers and the olives, heat through and taste for seasoning.

Meanwhile, season the fish steaks on both sides and dust them all over with flour. Heat the remaining oil in a large non-stick frying pan over a medium heat and sear the fish steaks for 2–3 minutes on each side. Using tongs, gently remove the swordfish from the pan and add it to the sauce. Cook for around 10 minutes. Take the fish out of the pan with tongs and set aside on a warm plate.

Add the potatoes to the pan, with a little more hot water if the sauce is very thick. Cook the potatoes for five minutes and then put the fish back into the pan. When the sauce is bubbling hot, serve straight away with the extra parsley on top.

sea bass cooked in a parcel with tuscan herbs

**SERVES
2 PEOPLE**

1 sprig of rosemary, leaves
   picked
½ teaspoon salt
¼ teaspoon freshly ground
   black pepper
1 fat garlic clove, peeled
600 g (1 lb 5 oz) whole sea
   bass, cleaned and scaled,
   or 2 sea bass fillets
1 lemon, ½ sliced into rings,
   and ½ cut into wedges,
   to serve
2 tablespoons extra-virgin
   olive oil

This very easy recipe was shown to us by Antonella Secciani, a chef at an *agriturismo*. She showed us how to wrap the fish in baking parchment and then in foil to ensure the precious flavours and juices don't escape. I have been cooking fish *al cartoccio* (see page 49) like this for years but have never been so bold with the flavours. However, it works brilliantly and I now make this dish with fillets if I can't get hold of a whole fish. The advantage of using fillets is that you don't need to bone the fish. Sea bream works perfectly if sea bass is hard to find.

Preheat the oven to 170°C (340°F/Gas 3). Make a *battuto* from the rosemary leaves, salt, pepper and garlic (see page 29). Rub this mixture over the skin and inside the cavity of the sea bass. Put the lemon slices in the belly of the fish, lay the fish on a large rectangle of baking parchment and drizzle over 1 tablespoon of the oil. Bring the long edges of the paper together and fold them over and over until you are about 5 cm (2 in) from the fish. Fold the short ends of the parcel up and inwards, a few times on each end. Wrap the fish parcel fairly tightly in some foil and lay it on a baking tray.

Cook the fish for 30–35 minutes, or until it feels firm to the touch. Open the parcel and check the fish is cooked through. If not, wrap it up again and put it back in the oven for a few minutes. When it is cooked, remove from the oven, unwrap and fillet the fish. Put the fish on a warm serving plate and pour over any juices from the parcel and drizzle with the remaining oil. Serve with the lemon wedges, some steamed potatoes, or sautéed potatoes with spring onions (scallions), spinach, chilli and garlic.

●

Variation:
To cook the recipe using fillets instead of whole fish, simply rub the *battuto* onto both sides of 2 fillets. Lay the lemon slices on top of one fillet and put the other fillet on top, skin facing outwards, as if you are re-assembling the fish. Follow the recipe as above, cooking the fillets for 14–17 minutes or until firm to the touch. Serve as above.

●

calf's liver with butter & sage

**SERVES
4 PEOPLE**

4 pieces calf's liver
(each approx. 200 g/7 oz)
salt and freshly ground
black pepper
plain (all-purpose) flour,
for dredging
4 tablespoons olive oil
4 garlic cloves, peeled
75 g (2½ oz) salted butter,
at room temperature
8 large fresh sage leaves

Did you know that calf's liver contains more vitamin C weight for weight than an apple? Nor did I. Calf's liver is a superfood, as it contains more nutrients (particularly if it's grass-fed) than most other foods, and we should be eating more of it. At our restaurants, calf's liver is the biggest-selling dish on our menu; I believe one of the reasons for this is that people don't like to cook it at home. Not wishing to diminish our sales, here is Giancarlo's tried and tested way to cook it to perfection.

Season the liver pieces on both sides with salt and pepper. Put some flour onto a plate and coat each piece of liver in flour on both sides. Heat the oil in a large non-stick frying pan over a medium heat, add the garlic cloves and fry for 1 minute. Increase the heat to high and add the floured liver pieces to the pan. Fry for 30 seconds on each side for medium-cooked liver or about 45 seconds on each side for well-done. If your pan isn't big enough, fry the liver in batches. Turn the heat down, add the butter and sage leaves to the pan, and continue cooking the liver until the butter has melted. Serve immediately, dressed with the butter, sage and garlic.

rabbit in white wine

**SERVES
6 PEOPLE**

1.6 kg (2 lb 5 oz) rabbit
(1 medium rabbit), jointed
into 12 pieces, or 1 chicken,
jointed
10 g (½ oz) rosemary leaves
1 fat garlic clove, peeled
1½ teaspoons salt
freshly ground black pepper
6 tablespoons extra-virgin
olive oil
400 ml (13 fl oz/1¾ cups)
dry white wine, such
as Vernaccia
50 g (2 oz) Kalamata or other
flavourful black olives
(stones in)

**This is a perfect example of Tuscan cooking where the meat becomes
so tender it falls off the bones and the sauce is rendered down to an
intense, umami-filled goo ready to be collected with bread or pieces
of rabbit. Do find your inner Tuscan peasant and eat it with your fingers.
This recipe is from the area of San Gimignano where they grow the
Vernaccia grapes to make their famous wine. Vernaccia wine is dry
and citrusy and suits the dish perfectly, so do hunt a bottle or two down.**

Trim any loose pieces of fat away from the jointed meat then wash the meat –
this will get rid of any small and loose bones. Dry on paper towel. Make
a *battuto* with the rosemary, garlic, salt and a few good twists of black pepper
(see page 29).

Heat the oil in a large non-stick frying pan over a medium heat. Add the
battuto and cook for just 1 minute, then add the rabbit pieces and fry for
10–15 minutes, turning the meat until it is lightly golden on all sides (watch
the pan to make sure the rabbit and *battuto* don't burn). When they are golden,
add the wine, cover with a lid and leave to cook over a medium heat for
30–40 minutes, or until the wine has evaporated down to around 100 ml
(3½ fl oz/scant ½ cup). If it is too watery, remove the lid and boil for longer.
Add the olives, cover the pan again, and cook for a further 10 minutes. Serve
with bread to mop up the juices, spinach, roast potatoes or steamed vegetables.

wild boar stew

**SERVES
8 PEOPLE**

1.6 kg (2 lb 5 oz) wild boar
    stewing steak, cut into
    3 cm (1¼ in) cubes
4 garlic cloves, peeled
25 g (1 oz) rosemary leaves
2 teaspoons salt
1 teaspoon coarsely ground
    black pepper
180 ml (6 fl oz/¾ cup)
    extra-virgin olive oil
500 ml (17 fl oz/2¼ cups)
    red wine
4 heaped tablespoons
    tomato purée (paste)
1.2–1.5 litres (2–2½ pints/
    5–6½ cups) Beef Bone Broth
    or Vegetable Stock (see page
    34 or 35), or boiling water

FOR THE MARINADE
1 onion, roughly chopped
1 long sprig of rosemary
1 carrot, roughly chopped
2 garlic cloves, peeled
1 teaspoon whole black
    peppercorns
1 teaspoon juniper berries
750 ml (25 fl oz/3 cups)
    red wine

Antonella Secciani, who showed us this recipe, cooks stews long and slow. She adjusts the heat to make sure the stew just quivers on the surface. When she was growing up she lived in a small village and there was a room, a *mattatoio* (a rudimentary butchers), where the wild boar were brought to clean, cut and distribute after a hunt. The best bit went to the person who shot it and the rest would be shared between them. It took around 20 men to kill one, maybe due to the fact that grappa was served frequently throughout the day!

Combine the marinade ingredients in a large bowl with the wild boar. Cover and leave to marinate overnight in the fridge. The following day, remove the meat from the marinade and discard everything but the meat.

Make a *battuto* from the garlic, rosemary, salt and pepper (see page 29). This time when making the *battuto*, as it is a large quantity, you can make it with the oil in a food processor, if you have one, to form a coarse paste.

Pour the oil and *battuto* into a large heavy-based saucepan and put it over a low heat. Add the marinated wild boar to the pan and stir through. Cook for 30 minutes or so until the water has evaporated from the meat.

Add the wine, increase the heat and bring to the boil. Continue to cook for about 10 minutes until the scent of wine has disappeared. Dissolve the tomato purée in the stock or water and pour into the pan. Cover and cook on a low heat for 2½–3 hours or until the meat is very tender. Add a little more stock or water from time to time if it looks dry. Remove the lid for the last hour of cooking, to concentrate the sauce. Taste and adjust the seasoning as necessary. Serve with soft polenta (see page 37), cannellini beans (see page 44) or mashed potato.

chicken meatloaf

**SERVES
6 PEOPLE**

2 tablespoons extra-virgin
  olive oil, plus extra for
  greasing and frying
500 g (1 lb 2 oz) minced
  (ground) chicken
1 white onion, peeled and
  finely chopped
100 g (3½ oz/generous ⅓ cup)
  ricotta
large handful of parsley,
  finely chopped
2 tablespoons fresh oregano,
  or 1 teaspoon dried oregano
100 g (3½ oz) finely grated
  Pecorino
2 teaspoons salt
¼ teaspoon freshly ground
  black pepper
2 eggs

TO SERVE
sprigs of oregano, thyme
  or rosemary (optional)

Inspired by the meatloaves and stuffed meats in the butcher's shops and market stalls of Tuscany, this is our recipe for an easy supper that our whole family loves. Serve it warm as it is, or with the Homemade Tomato Sauce on page 40. We even like it cold the following day with mayonnaise and a green salad. The mixture can also be used to make small patties for canapés, large ones resembling burgers, or to stuff vegetables (see page 190).

Preheat the oven to 180°C (350°F/Gas 4) and grease a 1 lb (22 × 12 × 6 cm/ 8½ × 5 × 2½ in) loaf tin with a little olive oil.

To make the meatloaf, mix all the ingredients together in a bowl. Heat 1 tablespoon of oil in a small non-stick frying pan. To test the flavour of the meatloaf, take a walnut-sized ball of the mixture, flatten it into a patty shape and fry it in the oil until cooked through. It should be firm to the touch and any juices should run clear when it is pierced with a skewer. Allow to cool for a couple of minutes, then taste for seasoning. (I have realised many a time that my mixture needs more oomph and have added more seasoning, more cheese or herbs at this point, so it is always good to test it.) Adjust the seasoning as necessary and spoon the mixture into the greased loaf tin.

Put the loaf tin into a roasting dish and fill the dish with cold water until it comes halfway up the tin, to make a bain marie. This will create steam in the oven which will prevent the meatloaf becoming dry while it cooks. Cook for 50 minutes–1 hour or until the meatloaf feels very firm to the touch or the internal temperature reaches 75–80°C (170–175°F) on a probe (meat) thermometer. The juices should run clear when pierced through to the centre.

Remove from the oven and allow to cool for 5 minutes in the tin, then turn the meatloaf out onto a warm serving platter with any juices from the tin poured over the loaf. I like to decorate it with fresh herbs to serve.

porcini & chestnut mushroom loaf

SERVES
4–6 PEOPLE

6 tablespoons extra-virgin olive oil, plus extra for greasing

30 g (1 oz) dried porcini mushrooms

100 g (3½ oz) stale crusty wheat or gluten-free bread

150 ml (5 fl oz/⅔ cup) milk

1 white onion, peeled and finely chopped

1 fat garlic clove, peeled and lightly crushed

900 g (2 lb) chestnut mushrooms, finely chopped

1½ teaspoons salt

a few twists of freshly ground black pepper

3 sprigs of thyme, leaves picked

1 teaspoon dried oregano

75 g (2½ oz) walnuts, chopped finely by hand or in a food processor

25 g (1 oz) grated Parmesan

2 eggs, beaten

200 g (7 oz) Homemade Tomato Sauce (see page 40) or Fresh Tomato Passata (see page 41)

FOR THE SAUCE

3 tablespoons extra-virgin olive oil

1 red onion, finely sliced into half moons

salt and freshly ground black pepper

175 ml (6 fl oz/¾ cup) red wine

200 ml (7 fl oz/generous ¾ cup) porcini stock from the dried mushrooms

2 tablespoons salted butter

Inspired by the amazing offerings at the markets of Tuscany, I developed this recipe with our friend Anna Hudson. The cooked mushrooms also make a wonderful pâté for crostini (see page 125). Do have patience when cooking them, as the flavours intensify with time.

Preheat the oven to 180°C (350°F/Gas 4). Line the base and the two long sides of a 1 lb (22 × 12 × 6 cm/8½ × 5 × 2½ in) loaf tin with a strip of folded foil, allowing it to protrude from the tin by around 5 cm (2 in) each side (this wide foil strip will act as handles to remove the loaf later). Grease the foil with olive oil.

Soak the dried mushrooms in a bowl of 400 ml (13 fl oz/1¾ cups) warm water and the bread in a separate bowl with the milk for about 10 minutes until soft.

Heat the oil in a large frying pan over a medium heat with 3 tablespoons of water. Add the onion and garlic and cook for 7–10 minutes or until soft. Meanwhile, drain the soaked porcini mushrooms (keep the soaking liquid). Add the porcini and chestnut mushrooms to the pan with the seasoning and herbs and cook over a high heat until the water has evaporated. Continue to cook, stirring frequently, until they start to catch on the bottom of the pan, then remove from the heat and transfer the mushrooms to a bowl. Chop them very finely by hand or in a food processor, keeping some coarse texture, then return them to the bowl. (This is the mushroom pâté – see page 125.)

Squeeze the bread and discard the milk. Crumble it into the bowl of mushrooms and add the walnuts, Parmesan and eggs and stir. Spoon into the greased tin and flatten the top with a spatula. Spoon over the tomato sauce. Put the tin into a roasting dish and fill the dish with cold water until it comes halfway up the loaf tin to make a bain marie. Cook for 30–40 minutes or until firm to the touch. Remove from the oven and leave in the tin for 5 minutes. Use the foil to remove the loaf from the tin and serve on a warm plate.

Meanwhile, make the sauce. Heat the oil in a frying pan over a low heat with 5 tablespoons of water, the onion, a good pinch of salt and a few twists of black pepper and cook for 20 minutes until the onion is translucent. Add a tablespoon or two more of water to keep them soft, if necessary (you don't want them to crispen up). Pour in the wine and let it evaporate over a low heat for 10 minutes to reduce the liquid by half. If there is sediment in the bowl from the mushrooms, drain the soaking liquid through a piece of paper towel in a sieve over a jug to remove it. Add the mushroom stock to the pan and turn up the heat to boil. Reduce the heat and let it bubble gently for 5 minutes. Add the butter and stir through. Taste and season if necessary. Remove from the heat and set aside until the loaf is ready. The sauce can be blended to make it thicker and smooth or left with the softened onion. Briefly reheat it and serve it in a warm jug with the loaf. The loaf is lovely with Vegetables Steamed in Paper (see page 237) or sautéed spinach (see page 38).

pork tenderloin with flavio's tuscan 'dust'

**SERVES
4–6 PEOPLE**

1 × 600 g (1 lb 5 oz) pork
    tenderloin
½ teaspoon fine sea salt
¼ teaspoon freshly
    ground black pepper
1 tablespoon chicken fat
    or extra-virgin olive oil

FOR THE DUST
2 teaspoons dried or
    fresh rosemary needles
1 teaspoon dried sage
    or 3 large fresh sage leaves
1 teaspoon fennel seeds,
    crushed (optional)

TO SERVE
Lentils with Soffritto
    (see page 229), to serve

This is our speedy version of an *arista*, an ancient dish made from loin of pork roast with rosemary and garlic. *Arista* comes from the Greek word *aristo*, meaning 'best'. Our son Flavio makes a Tuscan rub or 'dust' that can be used on potatoes, chicken or meat dishes such as this. The quantities given here make more rub than you need for this dish, but it will keep in the cupboard for as long as other dried herbs (see how to dry herbs on page 43). The rub can also be made with fennel seeds, which Giancarlo loves but Flavio doesn't – the choice is yours! Serve the tenderloin with the lentils on page 229.

Start by making the dust. If you are using dried herbs, crush them with the seeds (if using) with a pestle and mortar or a spice grinder. If using fresh herbs, finely chop them together with the seeds (if using) on a board with a sharp knife.

Evenly sprinkle 1 tablespoon of dust on the tenderloin over a piece of baking parchment with the salt and pepper. Trim away any tough silver skin from the tenderloin and roll it in the dust on the paper. Roll up the loin in the parchment, place it on a plate and set aside in the fridge for at least 30 minutes (or up to 8 hours).

Preheat the oven to 180°C (350°F/Gas 4). Remove the pork from the fridge and allow it to come to room temperature. Heat the chicken fat or oil in a large non-stick frying pan and, when hot, add the pork and brown it all over to seal in the juices. Transfer to a roasting tin and cook in the oven for 12–15 minutes or until it is firm to the touch. Remove from the oven and set aside, covered in foil and a tea towel (dish towel) to rest for 10 minutes. Cut into roughly 1 cm- (½ in-) thick slices and arrange on top of warm lentils, with any cooking juices poured over the meat.

slow-cooked beef stew with black peppercorns

**SERVES
8 PEOPLE**

120 ml (4 fl oz/½ cup)
extra-virgin olive oil
2 red onions, peeled and
finely sliced
1.2 kg (2 lb 10 oz) stewing beef
2 teaspoons salt
1½ teaspoons coarsely ground
black pepper
500 ml (17 fl oz/2¼ cups)
red wine
2 tablespoons whole
black peppercorns
polenta (see page 37),
to serve (optional)

Legend has it that the Tuscan brickmakers would take this to work for lunch, cooking it in the furnaces used to make terracotta tiles for the roof of the *Cathedrale di Santa Maria del Fiore* (known as the Duomo) in Florence between the 13th and 14th centuries. However, it is doubtful they could have afforded peppercorns so perhaps these were added in more recent times. This stew is often eaten with soft polenta or mashed potato or a *sformato* of cauliflower (see page 158). Traditionally, it would have been eaten with bread. This is Alfredo Bianchetti's recipe – he was a Florentine chef from this century who perfected the recipe over years of cooking it.

Preheat the oven to 170°C (340°F/Gas 3). Heat the oil in a large heavy-based ovenproof pan over a medium heat with 3 tablespoons of water. Add the onions and cook for about 10 minutes or until soft. When the onions are ready, add the meat, salt and ground pepper, and stir through. Continue to cook over a medium heat for about 30 minutes or until the water from the meat has evaporated. Pour in the wine and add the peppercorns, then cover with an ovenproof lid. Transfer the pan to the oven and cook for 2½–3 hours until the beef is soft. Take off the lid and bring the stew to the boil over a medium heat on the hob – the liquid should reduce until the sauce is soupy. Eat straight away with polenta (see page 37), or allow to cool and store in the fridge for up to 5 days, or chill and freeze for up to 3 months.

tuscan beef, porcini & chianti stew

**SERVES
8–10 PEOPLE**

15 g (½ oz) dried porcini
    mushrooms
300 ml (10 fl oz/1¼ cups)
    hot water
4 tablespoons extra-virgin
    olive oil
25 g (1 oz) salted butter
2 large white onions, peeled
    and cut finely into half moons
2 small celery stalks,
    finely chopped
1 large carrot, finely diced
1–2 teaspoons salt, to taste
2 bay leaves
½ teaspoon dried chilli flakes
800 g (1 lb 12 oz) diced
    braising steak
275 g (9½ oz) portobello
    mushrooms, roughly
    chopped
250 ml (8½ fl oz/1 cup) Chianti
    or other red wine, such
    as merlot
pinch of ground nutmeg

Frosty evenings, log fires and Chianti were created for this winter wonder. This beef stew is a family favourite of ours, which we serve with soft cheesy polenta (see page 37) and steamed kale for a hearty winter supper –and don't forget to drink the rest of the bottle of red wine with it!

This is a good opportunity to use the less-than-prime cuts of beef such as brisket, blade or skirt. The meat should be chopped into bite-sized pieces; depending on the size and cut, some pieces will soften more quickly than others, but this is a very forgiving stew packed with flavour. It will happily sit on a warm hob until you are ready to serve, or you can reheat small portions on the stove or in the microwave for last-minute meals.

Soak the dried porcini in the hot water for around 15 minutes or until soft. Heat the oil and butter in a large, heavy-based lidded pan and add the onions, celery, carrot, salt, bay leaves and chilli. Keep the heat low and fry for about 15 minutes or until the vegetables are tender. Add the braising steak, increase the heat to medium and fry for about 10 minutes or until browned all over.

Lift the porcini out of the soaking water with a slotted spoon or your fingers and roughly chop them. Reserve the water. Add both types of mushroom to the pan and stir through. After 5 minutes, add the wine, increase the heat and let it bubble for 2–3 minutes. Slowly pour the porcini water into the pan, being careful not to allow any sediment or grit from the bottom of the bowl to get into the pan. Add the nutmeg, stir again, and cover with the lid. Reduce the heat to a gentle simmer, until it is just bubbling, and continue to cook for 1½–2 hours, or until the meat is very tender and falls apart easily.

Every now and again, check the stew and add a little hot water if necessary. Let the water from the lid, when you lift it, drip back into the pan. If you find the stew watery, let it cook for the remainder of the time without the lid, to reduce the liquid. Serve straight away, or cool and store in a sealed container in the fridge for up to 5 days.

LA BISTECCA
FIORENTINA
(PAGE 212)

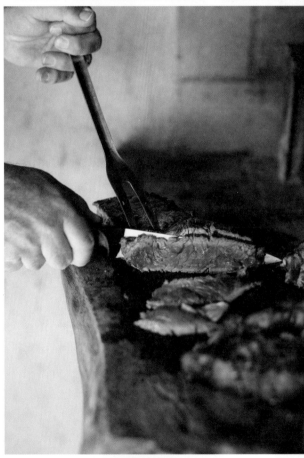

la bistecca fiorentina

SERVES
6–8 PEOPLE

1.2 kg (2 lb 6 oz) *Fiorentina*
salt and freshly ground
    black pepper

The Italians call this cut of beef steak *Fiorentina*, the English call it a T-bone, the Americans call it a Porterhouse. Whatever you call it, it is a huge slab of tender fillet and hunky sirloin surrounded with creamy fat that keeps it juicy as it is grilled on all sides. It is grilled briefly and served rare on wooden boards with grooves around the edges to catch the juices. In Tuscany's capital city of Florence, the smell of chargrilled steak wafts out of restaurants and the huge cuts are usually shown to the customers before they are cooked. A *Fiorentina* is large enough for two or more people to enjoy, and as the edges are seared brown and the centre is blue rare there is something for everyone.

Much of what gives flavour to meat is the breed of cattle from which it originates. In this case, the huge white cattle, the Chianina (named after the Chiana Valley in Tuscany where they have grazed for centuries, where Chianti wine is made) is the breed typically used for *bistecca Fiorentina*, which is traditionally grilled over an open fire. The Chianina are one of the oldest breeds and feature in Roman sculpture and artwork. Their meat is both tender and flavoursome, its well-marbled fat making it succulent and flavourful. Because of the size reached by the animals the steaks can easily exceed 2 kg (4 lb 6 oz). Each restaurant has a certificate to prove their steaks are Chianina; if they don't, it is likely they are not serving genuine Chianina.

Let the steak come to room temperature for 30 minutes. Meanwhile, fire up your grill or barbecue to hot and set a grill rack around 10 cm (4 in) away from the heat source. Season the meat generously all over (see opposite) and use a good pair of tongs to hold the steak.

Cook each side for 4 minutes for rare, or 6 minutes for just off rare. Then use the tongs to hold the steak upright on the grill and cook the edges for 5 minutes all the way around, including the bone side. This will help to drive the heat inside. Rest the steak for at least 10 minutes before serving (see the notes opposite).

Season generously

If you are going to cook your own *Fiorentina* (or any cut of steak), season it well, massaging salt and pepper into the flesh just before cooking. Many chefs prefer to salt after cooking or searing, but having done tests we've concluded that seasoning before or after cooking makes little difference to the finished steak. On my cooking courses many people ask why their steak doesn't taste like one cooked in a restaurant. Apart from the quality of the meat and hanging time, it is the fact that the hand of a chef will be more generous with the salt than that of a home cook. Simple as that. So don't spare the salt, this time.

How to tell when a steak is done

To tell when a steak is done to your liking, press the top of it while it is still in the pan or under the grill. The resistance to touch will demonstrate how it is cooked. You can compare the feeling to various parts of your hand, using this simple guide. Press your thumb and index finger together and prod the soft fleshy area at the base of your thumb with the index finger of your other hand. It will be soft to the touch like a 'rare' steak feels. Next, move your middle finger to touch your thumb and feel the point again – it will feel like a 'medium-rare' steak. The third finger will make it feel like 'medium' and the little finger like 'well done'.

Resting steak

Ideally, cooked meat should be rested for the same amount of time as it takes to cook. This is because when meat is cooked the blood rushes away from the surface to the inside of the meat, causing the outside to be dry. Allowing meat to rest means that the blood can become evenly distributed through the meat again, removing any dryness.

What to serve with your *bistecca Fiorentina*?

Lemon wedges, roast potatoes with spring onions (scallions) (see page 224) or freshly boiled cannellini beans with sage, olive oil, salt, and pepper and – of course – a good glass of a super Tuscan red wine.

contorni

I°CAT
£3.50 A Kg

vegetables

Tuscans cook vegetables with care and respect. They are never dressed with anything to embarrass or overwhelm their delicate flavours. In fact, vegetables are often scantily clad in nothing but a slick of young olive oil and a shimmer of salt. As an ex-vegetarian, I will pass on a tip from my travels in Italy: don't expect sumptuous vegetarian offerings for main courses. Instead, go straight to *contorni* and make a selection of dishes from there.

tomato & cucumber salad

SERVES
6 PEOPLE

½ small red onion, peeled
  and very finely diced
5 tablespoons best-quality
  extra-virgin olive oil
1 tablespoon red wine vinegar
salt and freshly ground
  black pepper
600 g (1 lb 5 oz) ripe, flavourful
  tomatoes (one type or a
  mixture of heritage, round
  or cherry)
2 sticks celery, finely sliced
small handful of celery leaves,
  roughly chopped
handful of parsley leaves,
  roughly chopped
15 medium basil leaves,
  roughly torn
½ long cucumber, peeled
  and thinly sliced

Salads are simple in Tuscany, usually consisting of a collection of the freshest vegetables in season from the *orto* (allotment) or the market. *Panzanella* is a tomato and cucumber salad with yesterday's bread soaked in water then crumbled into a salad dressed with vinegar and oil. However, unless you can get hold of Tuscan-style bread, which bounces back after soaking, it just isn't the same, so we haven't included it.

Giancarlo loves quartered tomatoes simply dressed with basil, oil and salt. He will eat them with scrambled eggs in the morning to a steak at night. My favourite way to eat tomatoes is in this salad.

Soak the sliced onion in a bowl of cold water for 15 minutes to mellow the flavour. Whisk the oil and vinegar together in a bowl and season lightly with a pinch of salt and black pepper. Cut away and discard the first slice of each tomato where it meets the stem. Cut the remaining flesh into 5 mm- (¼ in-) thick slices. There is no need to do this for cherry tomatoes – simply halve them around the equator rather than pole to pole. Drain the onions well in a sieve.

Put a layer of tomatoes onto a serving plate and scatter over a spoonful of celery and onions. Season lightly with a pinch of salt and pepper and a scattering of herbs. Pour over a little dressing. Top with a layer of cucumber and repeat with some more onions, herbs and dressing. Repeat until all the ingredients are used up and pour over any leftover dressing. Serve within 1 hour.

peas, bacon & onions

**SERVES
4–6 PEOPLE**

3 tablespoons extra-virgin
   olive oil
2 slices of bacon (smoked
   or unsmoked), cut into
   1 cm (½ in) strips
1 small white onion, peeled
   and finely chopped
1 × 400 g (14 oz) tin petits pois
   (net weight 265 g/9½ oz)
   or 250 g (9 oz) fresh peas,
   boiled until tender
salt and freshly ground
   black pepper

Imagine a glass jar of peas in Giancarlo's mother's *cantina* (pantry). The jar is full of summer's sweetest early young peas preserved in water, salt and a little sugar. On the jar is a handwritten label 'Piselli, Giugno 1955'. Now imagine a tin of peas from your nearest supermarket. Not quite the same idea? Actually, the contents are more or less the same; don't diss tinned peas – as a standby vegetable they are sweet and delicious! If fresh peas are in season and you like the therapeutic practise of podding, do use those instead.

Heat the oil in a saucepan over a medium heat. Add the bacon and onion, and sauté until the onion is soft and the bacon is cooked through. Add the tin of peas with half the liquid from the tin (discard the rest), or add the fresh boiled peas with a splash of cooking water. Heat through for around 5 minutes over a medium heat until the peas are hot. Season with salt and pepper to taste and serve straight away, or keep warm until ready to eat.

giancarlo's cannellini beans

**SERVES
6 PEOPLE**

4 tablespoons extra-virgin
   olive oil
2 garlic cloves, peeled
   and lightly crushed
5 sage leaves, or 2 sprigs
   of rosemary
500 g (1 lb 2 oz) cooked
   cannellini beans, drained
   (see page 44)
salt and freshly ground
   black pepper

We often show people how to prepare this store cupboard side dish. It's so simple but tastes amazing. Either cook the beans from scratch (see page 44) or open a couple of tins.

Heat the oil, garlic and herbs in a pan over a low heat for 3–5 minutes until you can smell the *aromi* (the flavours); take care they do not burn. Add the beans and some salt and pepper, and stir well. Cook for 5–10 minutes until the beans are heated through. If they start to dry out, add a little stock or hot water. Remove the herbs and garlic, and either leave the beans as they are or crush them briefly with a potato masher. Serve straight away with the oil from the pan.

Clockwise from top left: Giancarlo's Auntie Orlandina, Adelmo Caldesi (Giancarlo's father), Marietta Bellugi (Giancarlo's mother) and cousins from America; Giancarlo's parents; Giancarlo and his brother with their parents; Adelmo Caldesi; Giancarlo's parents with neighbours Elide, Nello and Monica; Giancarlo as a little boy

potatoes & leeks or spring onions

**SERVES
4–6 PEOPLE**

1.2 kg (2 lb 10 oz) new or
  roasting potatoes, left whole
  if small, or peeled and
  roughly chopped into
  3 cm (1¼ in) cubes
4 tablespoons extra-virgin
  olive oil
25 g (1 oz) salted butter
1 large leek, trimmed and cut
  into half-moons around 1 cm
  (½ in) wide, or 1 bunch of
  spring onions (scallions),
  trimmed and roughly
  chopped
salt and freshly ground
  black pepper
25 g (1 oz) grated Parmesan
  or Pecorino (optional)
small handful of parsley,
  roughly chopped, to serve

You can use any type of potato for this. The cheese is an optional extra but we love it; I would perhaps leave it out if you are serving it with fish. This is a great side dish but also works well as a main course (or even a breakfast) to fill up hungry teenagers, with a couple of poached eggs on the side if you fancy.

Boil the potatoes in a large saucepan of salted water until tender. Depending on their size, they will take 15–20 minutes.

When the potatoes are done, drain and set aside. Heat the oil and butter in a large non-stick frying pan over a gentle heat. Add the leeks or spring onions and the potatoes, and season with salt and pepper. Cook for 10–15 minutes until the onions soften and the potatoes start to brown. Scatter over the cheese (if using) and continue to cook for a further 3–5 minutes, stirring the cheese into the potatoes. It will start to brown and catch in the pan (these browned bits are delicious). Tip the potato mixture into a warm serving dish, scatter with the parsley and serve.

sautéed leaves with chilli & garlic

SERVES
4–6 PEOPLE

3 tablespoons extra-virgin
    olive oil
2 garlic cloves, peeled and
    lightly crushed
fresh red chilli, to taste,
    roughly sliced
generous pinch of salt and
    freshly ground black pepper
200 g (7 oz) cooked and drained
    green leaves (see page 38),
    such as spinach, chard,
    curly kale or cavolo nero,
    roughly chopped

Simple sautéed green leaves are on every *contorni* menu in Italian restaurants. They are sometimes eaten as part of antipasti or to go with grilled meats or fish. I could eat a plate of these for breakfast, lunch or dinner, on their own or with a poached egg on top. For how to cook greens, see page 38.

Heat the oil with the garlic, chilli, salt and pepper in a large frying pan over a low heat for 2–3 minutes until you can smell the flavours in the oil, but watch carefully to make sure they don't burn. Add the cooked leaves and fry for about 5 minutes, stirring constantly. Taste and adjust the seasoning as necessary. Serve in a warm bowl.

●

Note: If you are using baby spinach leaves you can toss them with the oil, garlic and chilli in the pan until softened without cooking them first. Season to taste.

●

lentils with soffritto

SERVES
6–8 PEOPLE

FOR THE SOFFRITTO
4 tablespoons extra-virgin
 olive oil, plus extra to serve
1 small carrot, finely diced
1 celery stalk, finely diced
1 small onion, peeled
 and finely diced
1 garlic clove, peeled
 and lightly crushed
1 sprig of rosemary
salt and freshly ground
 black pepper, to taste

FOR THE LENTILS
250 g (9 oz) small brown lentils
150 g (5 oz) Fresh Tomato
 Passata (see page 41),
 or tinned plum tomatoes,
 puréed
600 ml (20 fl oz/2½ cups)
 Vegetable or Chicken Stock
 (see page 35 or 32),
 or hot water
salt and freshly ground
 black pepper
4–5 sprigs of parsley,
 leaves and fine stalks
 finely chopped, tough
 stalks discarded

This is the Italian way to cook small brown lentils. They are a great earthy, textural backdrop for fish, pork or chicken. The only difference between lentils eaten this way as a side or as a soup is that a little more liquid is added for soup. Sometimes we add a pinch of chilli flakes if we want a little heat, or a handful of soft chestnuts if we want another texture in the dish. To make this quickly, use a 400 g (14 oz) tin of pre-cooked lentils. Drain the water from them and only add 100 ml (3½ fl oz/scant ½ cup) of stock to the dish.

Pick over and wash the lentils, then drain and set aside. Heat a saucepan over a gentle heat and make the *soffritto* (see page 28). Allow to cook for about 10 minutes. When the vegetables are soft, add the lentils and stir through. Add the tomatoes and enough stock or water to cover the lentils (you may not need all of it) and continue to cook for 45 minutes–1 hour, or until the lentils are soft. Remove a third of the lentils and pass them through a *passatutto* (food mill) or sieve, or use a stick blender to purée them. Discard the skins of the lentils that are left behind. Return the purée to the pan and bring to the boil. Adjust the seasoning as necessary and serve warm, scattered with parsley.

roasted vegetables

SUMMER ROASTED VEGETABLES

2 red (bell) peppers, quartered, cored and seeds removed

2 courgettes (zucchini), cut into 1 cm (½ in) slices

1 large aubergine (eggplant), cut into 1 cm (½ in) slices

2 medium red onions, peeled and cut into 12 wedges

salt and freshly ground black pepper

5–6 tablespoons extra-virgin olive oil (enough to coat the vegetables)

3 garlic cloves, skin left on

4–5 sprigs of fresh thyme and/or rosemary

WINTER ROASTED VEGETABLES

1 small cauliflower, cut into bite-sized florets

2 medium red onions, peeled and cut into 12 wedges

⅓ celeriac, cut into wedges similar to the size of the onions

2 medium carrots, cut into batons the size of your little finger

1 celery stalk, cut into 2 cm (¾ in) slices

1 leek, trimmed and cut into 2 cm (¾ in) slices

salt and freshly ground black pepper

5–6 tablespoons extra-virgin olive oil (enough to coat the vegetables)

3 garlic cloves, skin left on

4–5 few sprigs of fresh thyme and/or rosemary

Verdure alla griglia are usually slices of courgette (zucchini), aubergine (eggplant), (bell) pepper, asparagùs and sometimes onions and tomatoes cooked quickly on a grill. Thin slices of courgette, red onion and radicchio can be dry-fried in a frying or a griddle pan, which is what we have done in the photograph opposite. However, they do take a while and you have to watch them carefully and turn them frequently so that they don't bur. My favourite way to grill them is dry-grilled over a proper charcoal fire then dressed with good olive oil and salt. But since we don't have an open fire in our kitchen, we pan- or oven-roast them instead. They are wonderful on their own, as *contorni* or as the base for a sauce instead of pasta.

This versatile recipe can be used with any vegetable you have that roasts well. As Tuscans follow the seasons, naturally soft vegetables such as aubergines, courgettes and cherry tomatoes are available at the same time of year – summer. They roast quickly and pair well. Similarly, winter vegetables such as cauliflowers, celery, celeriac and carrots make a wonderful winter roast and have slightly longer cooking times, so do bear this in mind. Onions, celery, herbs and garlic go well with both.

Preheat the oven to 200°C (400°F/Gas 6). Put the vegetables in a large bowl with a big pinch of salt, a few twists of pepper and the oil, and mix thoroughly with your hands. Lay them on a baking tray in a single layer. This is important – if they overlap or are piled on top of each other, the vegetables will steam rather than roast, and become soggy. Squash the garlic cloves lightly with the flat side of a large knife to release their flavour. Add them to the tin. Tuck the herbs under the vegetables to stop them burning.

Roast for 25–35 minutes, or until the vegetables are starting to brown around the edges and are just cooked through. Serve straight away or allow to cool to room temperature

split broad beans with fried onions

**SERVES
4–6 PEOPLE**

250 g (9 oz) dried split
    broad (fava) beans
seed oil, for shallow frying
1 medium white or red onion,
    peeled and finely sliced
    into half-moons
salt and freshly ground
    black pepper
1 tablespoon best-quality
    extra-virgin olive oil

We have to say a huge thank you to the Anonimo Toscano, the anonymous Tuscan chef who wrote his recipes down in a book in the 1300s. This extract is taken from his book:
    'Split broad [fava] beans, washed in hot water, set them to boil; and when they have boiled, wash them well a second time, and set them to boil in enough water to cover them and protect them from smoke. And when they are well cooked, stir them with a stick; then dilute them with cold water, or white wine instead, so that they are well made. Then make them into a pottage, and add oil, with fried onions; and serve it.'
    For an nutritious and comforting side dish, do hunt down a packet of these dried and split broad beans. They were a staple diet in Tuscany's poorer history (as you can see in the 14th century), and in ours too in the UK since the Iron Age. Although they are grown in the UK, most are shipped abroad. In my opinion they are well worth resurrecting in our dishes and are easy to buy in the UK from the wonderfully-named Hodmedod.

Pick over the beans to get rid of any stones or shells. Cover the beans with cold water in a medium saucepan and put over a high heat. Bring to the boil, then reduce the heat and simmer for 40–50 minutes or until the beans can be easily squashed against the side of a pan with a wooden spoon. They will become softer the longer they cook. Add a little hot water during cooking if the beans start to look dry.

Meanwhile, heat some seed oil in a high-sided frying pan and fry the onion until crisp. Lift the onion out of the oil with a slotted spoon and drain on paper towel.

Either let the beans boil to a pulp or pottage for a further 10–15 minutes, as the Anonymous Tuscan suggested, and mash with a potato masher, or eat them while they still have some bite but are cooked through. Season the beans to taste, and serve them topped with the fried onions and drizzled with the olive oil.

white cabbage, fennel & onions with saffron

SERVES
4–6 PEOPLE

2 tablespoons extra-virgin
   olive oil
1 small white onion, peeled
   and sliced into half-moons
1 fat fennel bulb
500 g (1 lb 2 oz) (approx. ½)
   white cabbage
salt and freshly ground
   black pepper
100 ml (3½ fl oz/scant ½ cup)
   white wine
25 g (1 oz) salted butter
½ –1 teaspoon saffron strands

This is another extract from the book by an anonymous Tuscan chef in the 1300s, which inspired this glorious dish of golden cabbage and fennel flavoured with the heady scent of saffron strands, a favourite spice in the wealthy households of the Middle Ages.

'To make white cabbages, well cooked. Take stalks of cabbage, and clean them well, so that nothing is left of the leaves; and cut them at the softest part of the head: and when the pot has come to a boil, with oil and water inside, add said stalks, or rather the white parts of the cabbages, and add fennel bulbs, and let all of it boil until it is rather thick. And if you want, you can put in oil, or meat or capon broth, pepper, ground spices, beaten eggs, saffron for colour; and give it to your Lord.'

Heat the oil in a large non-stick frying pan over a low heat, add the onion and fry for 5 minutes. Add 3 tablespoons of water and continue to cook over a low heat for a further 10 minutes until soft.

Meanwhile, clean the fennel bulb and cut it into quarters. Discard the tough leaves from the outside and cut away the woody centres. Cut the cabbage into wedges similar in size to the fennel, also discarding the woody stem. Put both vegetables into a large saucepan of boiling salted water and cook for 7–10 minutes or until just soft when pierced with a skewer.

Lift the cabbage and fennel out of the water with a slotted spoon (keep the cooking water) and add them to the onion in the frying pan. Pour in the wine and let it reduce over a low heat for about 10 minutes, or until the smell of alcohol has completely disappeared. Do be patient here: it will sweeten the dish. Add 200 ml (7 fl oz/generous ¾ cup) of the vegetable cooking water, the butter and a ½ teaspoon of the saffron. Bring to the boil, then reduce the heat and cook for around 15 minutes, shaking the pan occasionally. Taste and adjust the seasoning, and add more saffron as necessary.

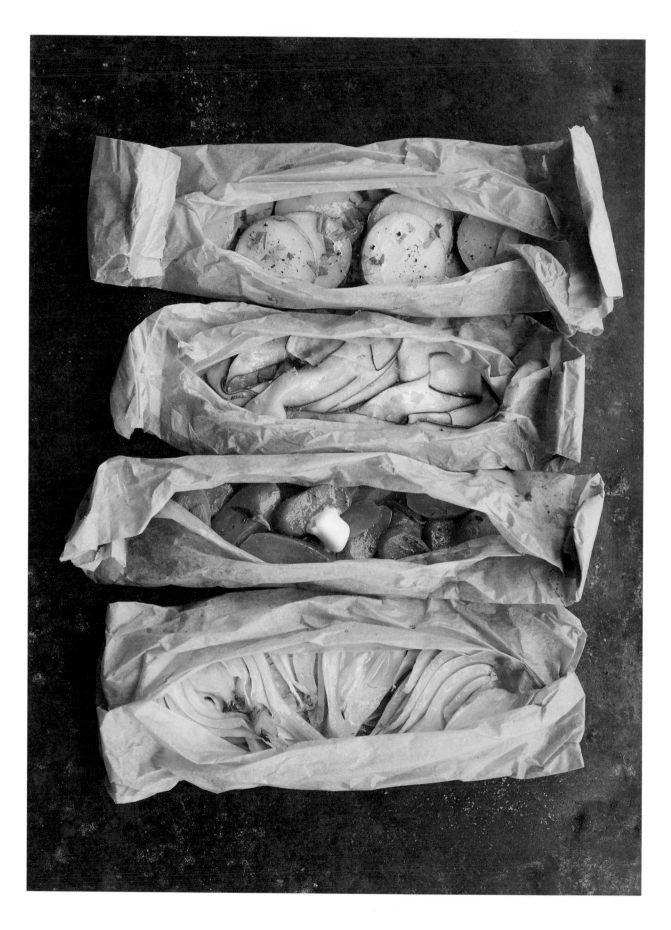

vegetables steamed in paper

selection of fennel, potatoes, carrots, courgettes (zucchini), cauliflower and (bell) peppers, cut into bite-sized pieces

These steamed vegetables will match the subtle and delicate flavours of fish or roast chicken, or are more than worthy of a lunch on their own. The flavour of the vegetables is concentrated and any juices stay in the paper. They are typically served completely plain or with a little seasoning and a drizzle of good-quality olive oil. Their intense flavour means you hardly need any salt, so go easy with seasoning.

I have been playing around with the flavours, since I am not good at leaving something simple alone! I like to add herbs and spices, leave some unseasoned, or add a knob of butter to the parcel – some of my favourites are courgettes (zucchini) wrapped with a splash of olive oil and a sprig of tarragon; carrots and leeks together in a parcel with nutmeg, black pepper, a small pinch of salt and a knob of butter; and potatoes and parsley or fennel with a few fennel seeds. Happy experimenting!

Preheat the oven to 180°C (350°F/Gas 4). Wrap the cut vegetables in baking parchment, following the instructions for cooking *al cartoccio* on page 49. Bake in the oven for 7–30 minutes, depending on the vegetable, or until cooked. The more watery, soft vegetables take less time than firm carrots and potatoes, for example (and the finer you cut them the quicker they will cook). You can press the top of the parcel to feel the give in the vegetables. Here are some examples of timings and flavour suggestions.

Courgettes (zucchini)
Thinly sliced, on their own.
7–10 minutes. Dress with your
best olive oil after cooking.

Green beans
With a splash of extra-virgin olive
oil and a pinch of salt and pepper.
12 minutes.

Shredded savoy cabbage
With salted butter and pepper.
8–10 minutes.

Potatoes
Cut into 1 cm (½ in) discs on their own.
20 minutes. Dress with salt, pepper
and butter after cooking.

Cauliflower florets
With nutmeg and butter.
15 minutes.

Carrot batons and chopped leeks
With salted butter and tarragon.
20–35 minutes.

dolci

desserts

'There is a *dolce* (dessert) for every month of the year,' our chef friend Antonella told me. From the spicy panforte from Siena (see Antonella's recipe on page 246), traditionally eaten at Christmas, to the stunning *schiacciata* cakes (see page 73) in every Florentine cake shop window in the run-up to Carnevale in February, the summer combinations of fresh fruits known as *macedonia* (see page 259) to the *pan con santi*, 'bread for the saints', made for Halloween, there is always a cake on offer to cheer the soul.

Sugar or chocolate was a rare treat when Giancarlo was growing up and desserts were generally made for a festival or, if you were lucky, each Sunday. Giancarlo remembers that when his family fired up the outside oven to cook bread once a fortnight, his mother would make a cake to take advantage of the hot coals.

Fresh seasonal fruits such as an apples, grapes, berries, cherries or bright orange persimmons are generally served at the end of a meal. Cheese is eaten at the beginning and instead of dessert (see our ideas for cheese on page 131). Figs and melons are also served at the beginning of a meal with salty prosciutto.

Ice cream and semifreddo are not generally made at home. Instead, the Tuscans prefer to dress up and take their evening walk, the *passeggiata*, which invariably ends at a bar or local ice cream shop – the *gelateria*. Simple sponge cakes and plain biscuits are designed for dunking and served with bitter espresso or the sweet wine Vin Santo. *Torrone*, the white nougat studded with nuts, and *cantuccini* are available in every patisserie and often given as presents when dining out. There are flamboyant desserts such as *zuppa Inglese*, inspired by English trifle and made with the bright pink Alchermes liqueur, or *zuccotto* made in a mould with ricotta, chocolate and sponge. This chapter features our favourite desserts, which we believe fit into a modern kitchen, don't take hours to make or require specialist equipment.

sweet swiss chard tart

SERVES
10–12 PEOPLE

FOR THE PASTRY
200 g (7 oz/1⅔ cups) '00' flour
200 g (7 oz) chilled butter, cubed
1 egg
100 g (3½ oz/scant ⅔ cup)
    caster (superfine) sugar
1 level teaspoon baking powder
finely grated zest of ½ lemon

FOR THE FILLING
50 g (2 oz) walnuts,
    roughly chopped
50 g (2 oz/⅓ cup) pine nuts
600 g (1 lb 5 oz) Swiss chard
    leaves and thin, tender
    stalks, or 300 g (10½ oz)
    spinach leaves and tender
    stalks, roughly chopped
pinch of salt
10 g (½ oz) salted or unsalted
    butter, cubed
500 g (1 lb 2 oz/2 cups) ricotta,
    drained
100 g (3½ oz/ generous ¾ cup)
    raisins
75 g (2½ oz/⅓ cup) caster
    (superfine) sugar
1 teaspoon ground cinnamon
    (optional)
finely grated zest of ½ lemon
ice cream, cream or Saffron
    Custard (see page 244),
    to serve

Long before anyone put beetroot (beets) into a chocolate cake and claimed vegetables in puddings a modern invention, the Lucchese were putting Swiss chard in a sweet tart of crumbly *pasta frolla* (shortcrust pastry) filled with ricotta, dried fruit and nuts, sugar and lemons.

At Franca Buonamici's house, the old grey parrot whistled and entertained us while we set to work making this traditional recipe from Lucca. Franca told me that after World War II, there was great poverty in the area and this tart was only made for a treat once in a while. The *contadini* (peasant farmers) had a lot of vegetables to hand, which were used to pad out *dolci* such as this. Pine nuts and raisins were used sparingly as they were expensive. Once a week, her family would light the big outdoor oven and make this tart, bake bread and cook other dishes from the neighbours. She told me it was a wonderful time – a party when everyone came together and enjoyed a once-a-week 'bake off' in the 1950s.

To make the pastry, put the flour and butter in a bowl and rub the butter into the flour with your fingertips until the mixture resembles fine breadcrumbs. Add the egg and the remaining ingredients and mix again to blend (make the pastry in a food processor if you prefer). Form the pastry into a ball, wrap it in cling film (plastic wrap) and leave it to rest in the fridge for 1 hour.

Preheat the oven to 180°C (350°F/Gas 4) and line a 24 × 3 cm (10 × 1¼ in) tart tin with baking parchment so that it protrudes above the edge of the dish by 2 cm (¾ in) (see page 46 for tips on how to make a cartouche).

To make the filling, put the walnuts and pine nuts in a roasting tray and toast them in the oven for 5 minutes. Remove and set aside to cool. Put the Swiss chard or spinach leaves in a pan with a little water, the salt and butter, cover and cook until soft and tender (Swiss chard will take longer than spinach). Once soft, drain and leave until cool enough to handle. Squeeze the leaves really well between your hands to rid them of excess water. Put the leaves on a board and chop them finely with a sharp knife. When cool, mix them in a bowl with the remaining ingredients. Taste and adjust the flavour with more cinnamon (if using) or lemon zest as necessary.

Remove the pastry from the fridge, unwrap it, roll it out to a thickness of around 5mm (¼ in) and use it to line the tart tin. Prick the base of the pastry with a fork and spoon in the filling mixture, smoothing the surface with a fork or palette knife. Trim away the excess pastry. Roll out the leftovers and cut strips about 1 cm (½ in) wide with a pastry wheel cutter or a knife. Create a lattice pattern on the top of the tart with the strips. Bake for around 45 minutes or until lightly browned.

Remove the tart from the oven and leave it to cool in the tin, then serve with ice cream, cream or Saffron Custard (see page 244).

apple cake with saffron custard

SERVES
10 PEOPLE

125 g (4 oz) softened
    salted butter, plus extra
    for greasing if required
180 g (6¼ oz/generous ¾ cup)
    caster (superfine) sugar
3 medium eggs
225 g (8 oz/generous 1¾ cups)
    self-raising flour
2 level teaspoons
    baking powder
2 teaspoons vanilla extract
finely grated zest of 1 lemon
2 large dessert apples,
    peeled and finely sliced
    (approx. 350 g/12 oz)
25 g (1 oz) nuts, such as flaked
    almonds, pine nuts
    or walnuts
25 g (1 oz) apricot jam
1 tablespoon icing
    (confectioners') sugar,
    to serve

FOR THE CUSTARD
1 teaspoon good-quality
    saffron strands
500 ml (17 fl oz/2¼ cups)
    whole (full-fat) milk
3 egg yolks
25 g (1 oz) caster (superfine)
    sugar
10 g (½ oz) cornflour
    (cornstarch)

We ate this delightfully light apple cake at Trattoria I Barberi in Siena. Tucked away on a side street slightly out of the centre of the town, the trattoria is well worth the walk to discover Chef Nicola's cooking. To make the cake gluten-free, substitute the wheat flour for cornflour (cornstarch).

The custard is flavoured with saffron, obtained from the stamens of the crocus flower. It takes around 125,000 flowers to produce 1 kg (2 lb 3 oz) of saffron, hence it is actually worth more per kilo than gold today. The fields around San Gimignano were full of flowers in the Middle Ages and saffron was known as 'red gold'. The profits from the production helped fund the town's famous towers. Saffron is being grown again in Tuscany thanks to the slow food movement.

Preheat the oven to 170°C (340°F/Gas 3) and line a 20 cm (8 in) cake tin with baking parchment (or grease it with butter).

Cream the butter and sugar together in a large bowl with an electric whisk or in a stand mixer until light and fluffy. Add the eggs, one at a time, and whisk again for 10 minutes until the mixture is light and fluffy again. Add the flour, baking powder, vanilla extract and lemon zest to the bowl and whisk together. Fold in the sliced apples with a large spatula and spoon the batter into the lined (or greased) tin. Level the surface with the spatula.

Bake in the oven for 40–45 minutes or until a skewer inserted into the middle of the cake comes out clean. Remove the cake from the oven and allow to cool for 5 minutes in the tin, then gently remove the cake from the tin and transfer it to a wire rack to cool, top facing up.

Toast the nuts in a dry frying pan until lightly golden. Put the jam in a small bowl and stir in 1 tablespoon of very hot water to loosen it. Spread the jam over the cake using a pastry brush, then scatter the toasted nuts around the rim of the cake, creating a border of about 5 cm (2 in). Sift the icing sugar over the nuts to serve.

For the custard, soak the saffron strands in 3 tablespoons of just-boiled water in a heatproof cup. Heat the milk in a medium saucepan until warm. Meanwhile, whisk the egg yolks, sugar and cornflour in a bowl. Whisk 1 ladleful of the warmed milk into the egg yolk mixture, then pour this mixture into the saucepan of milk, and add the saffron strands and their soaking water. Stir with a whisk continuously for a few minutes until the mixture thickens, then remove from the heat and serve with the cake.

mascarpone cheesecake alla port ellen clan

**SERVES
12 PEOPLE**

FOR THE BASE
100 g (3½ oz) unsalted butter
200 g (7 oz) cantuccini,
    digestive biscuits or oats

FOR THE FILLING
1 large egg
180 g (6¼ oz/generous ¾ cup)
    caster (superfine) sugar
500 g (1 lb 2 oz) mascarpone
    or cream cheese
500 g (1 lb 2 oz) ricotta
20 g (¾ oz) cornflour
    (cornstarch)
1 teaspoon vanilla extract,
    or seeds scraped from
    1 vanilla pod
juice of 1 lemon
200 ml (7 fl oz/generous ¾ cup)
    double (heavy) cream

FOR THE BERRY SAUCE
300 g (10½ oz) strawberries
200 g (7 oz) raspberries
3 tablespoons caster
    (superfine) sugar

This bizarrely named restaurant in Lucca run by Alessandro Sartoni is just lovely. Although most of their food sticks firmly to Lucchese traditions the exception is this indulgent mash-up of the two cultures of Italy and the US.

Preheat the oven to 150°C (300°F/Gas 2). Line a flan tin with baking paper (see page 46 for tips on how to make a cartouche). Melt the butter in a small saucepan over a medium heat until it is just melted. Pour into a blender or food processor and blend with the biscuits or oats. Spread this into the lined tin to form the base for the cheesecake. Put into the freezer for 30 minutes to set.

To make the filling, mix together the egg and sugar well in a stand mixer with a whisk attachment or an electric whisk. After they are well blended, whisk in the cheeses, cornflour, vanilla extract or seeds, lemon and cream. Spread this mixture over the chilled biscuit base and flatten out. Cook the cheesecake for 55 minutes. Remove from the oven and allow to cool.

Meanwhile, make the berry sauce by putting all the ingredients into a frying pan and briefly cook them over a medium heat for 5 minutes or until the berries start to soften. Remove from the heat and allow to cool before serving with the cheesecake.

antonella's panforte

SERVES
10–12 PEOPLE

100 g (3½ oz/scant 1 cup)
   '00' flour, plus extra for tin
   and jar
150 g (5 oz/1 cup) almonds,
   skin on
125 g (4 oz/generous ½ cup)
   caster (superfine) sugar
3 tablespoons mild honey
150 g (5 oz) mixture of candied
   cedro and/or candied orange
   peel, finely diced
1 teaspoon vanilla extract
¼ teaspoon ground cinnamon

FOR THE SPICE RUB
1 teaspoon icing
   (confectioners') sugar
¼ teaspoon finely ground
   black peppercorns
¼ teaspoon coriander seeds
¼ teaspoon ground cinnamon
pinch of finely grated nutmeg

Panforte (meaning 'strong bread') is found in all Sienese patisserie shops. It is a firm, chewy cake packed with nuts and spices. It is thought to date back to the 13th century as documents show it was given by traders to monks and nuns as a form of tax. Spice, although hugely expensive and exotic, was traded in Siena at the time through connections with the Middle East. It has taken Stefano Borella (a chef at our cookery school) and me years to be able to make a *panforte* that we are happy with, so a massive thank you to Antonella Secciani for sharing her precious recipe with us.

In 1879, Queen Margherita of Savoy paid a visit to Siena and a local spice seller made a version of the *panforte* cake with a white layer of vanilla-flavoured sugar on top in her honour, instead of black pepper; this is still available today. There are also darker versions with cocoa powder, others with walnuts, dried figs and many more. Every *panforte*-maker has their own secret blend of *panforte* spices and they never give away their recipes. Antonella's recipe is simple but you can experiment by adding pinches of ground black pepper, nutmeg, coriander, cloves and ginger. The spice rub is not essential but I rather like the hint of peppery heat that it gives.

Preheat the oven to 180°C (350°F/Gas 4). Line a 20 cm (8 in) cake tin with baking parchment and sprinkle a little flour over it. Put a little extra flour on a small plate and set aside.

Get a heavy-bottomed glass jar ready. Put the almonds on a baking tray and roast them for 5 minutes until they start to darken in colour and the skins start to crack. Remove from the oven and set aside. Leave the oven on.

Put the sugar, 2 tablespoons of water and honey into a saucepan and place over a medium–high heat for 5–7 minutes until the mixture reaches 105°C (221°F) on a sugar thermometer, or until the mixture is gently bubbling. Add the remaining ingredients to the pan, including the toasted almonds, and stir for 3 minutes. It will be tough to stir but it is important to warm up the flour, so keep stirring until the time is up. Spoon the mixture into the lined tin.

Dip the bottom of the glass jar into the flour on the plate and use it to bash the mixture down and flatten it into the tin. Do this quickly before it sets. Transfer the *panforte* to the oven and bake for 10 minutes, then remove and set aside to cool.

When cool, remove the *panforte* from the tin and peel off the baking parchment. Combine the ingredients for the spice rub in a bowl. Scatter it over the *panforte* to coat it evenly on both sides. It will keep if dry and covered at room temperature for a couple of weeks. Serve in small slices as it is very rich.

chestnut pancakes filled with ricotta & lemon

SERVES
6 PEOPLE

FOR THE PANCAKE BATTER
2 medium eggs
pinch of salt
pinch of sugar
125 g (4 oz/ 1¾ cups)
   chestnut flour
250–275 ml (8½–9½ fl oz/
   1–1¼ cups) whole (full-fat)
   milk
extra-virgin olive oil or lard,
   for frying

FOR THE FILLING
50 g (2 oz/generous ⅓ cup)
   raisins
25 ml (1 fl oz) rum
500 g (1 lb 2 oz/2 cups)
   ricotta, drained
100 g (3½ oz) cooked and
   peeled vacuum-packed
   chestnuts
2 tablespoons honey
2 teaspoons finely chopped
   rosemary needles
finely grated zest of ½ lemon

TO SERVE
runny honey, to drizzle
small handful of rosemary
   leaves, finely chopped
50 g (2 oz) crumbled toasted
chestnuts or toasted pine nuts

Necci (chestnut pancakes) are traditionally made in the north of Tuscany where chestnut trees proliferate. When wheat flour was sparse, chestnuts were dried and ground to use instead. Chestnut flour is used to make *castagnaccio*, a traditional flat cake decorated with pine nuts and rosemary. We took the decoration from this and paired it with *necci* to make this delicious dessert.

The naturally sweet, nutty flavour of chestnut flour makes perfect pancakes, which can be made in advance, kept well covered in the fridge, then heated quickly in a microwave or wrapped in foil to reheat in the oven. They are gluten-free and low in sugar (at least they are until our son Giorgio spreads his with Nutella and Giancarlo adds slices of banana). For an everyday recipe you could leave out the chestnuts, raisins and rum filling, but for a dinner party go the whole hog: the finished plates look very pretty with the rosemary and pine nuts.

To make the pancake batter, whisk the eggs in a bowl with the salt, sugar and flour. Gradually add 250 ml (8½ fl oz/1 cup) of the milk until you have a very smooth batter the consistency of runny, single (light) cream. Add a little more milk if necessary. Let the batter stand at room temperature for around 15 minutes. It can be made the day before and kept in the fridge, covered.

Meanwhile, combine the filling ingredients in a bowl and adjust the flavour with more lemon, honey and rosemary, to taste.

While you fry the pancakes leave a whisk in the bowl, as you need to stir the mixture thoroughly each time you use it. Wipe a 25 cm (10 in) non-stick frying pan with a thin layer of oil (using a potato – see Florentine Pancakes on page 189 – or a piece of paper towel) and, when hot, pour in 50 ml (2 fl oz/¼ cup) of batter with a ladle or small measuring jug, swirling it around the pan to coat the base evenly. Fry the pancake, flipping it over after 2–3 minutes or when one side is lightly browned, cook the other side, then transfer it to a plate. Fry the rest of the batter in the same way, stacking the pancakes on the plate as you make them. Keep them warm.

Spread 2 heaped tablespoons of the ricotta filling over half of each pancake and fold them in half and then half again. Serve straight away, drizzled with a little extra honey and sprinkled with the rosemary and crumbled chestnuts or pine nuts.

apricot & frangipane cake

SERVES
8 PEOPLE

125 g (4 oz/generous ½ cup) caster (superfine) sugar
320 g (11½ oz) fresh or tinned (and drained) apricots, stoned and halved
100 g (3½ oz) softened unsalted butter
200 g (7 oz/2 cups) ground almonds (almond meal)
2 eggs
2 level teaspoons baking powder
1 teaspoon vanilla extract
finely grated zest of 1 lemon
whipped cream or Saffron Custard (see page 244), to serve

Frangipane dates back to the 1500s, when the young Florentine Catherine de' Medici married King Henry II of France when they were both just 14. According to William Curley, the British patissier, she brought a brigade of chefs with her, including Popelini, who introduced many Italian recipes to the French court. He tried to emulate her favourite polenta with local ingredients. He used ground almond (almond meal), sugar, eggs and butter and she loved it. At the time, a perfume called Frangipani, named after the Marquis Frangipani, was fashionable. Catherine christened the delicacy after him as the scent of the almond cream reminded her of it. This cake has now become one of Giancarlo's favourites as it is gluten-free.

Preheat the oven to 170°C (340°F/Gas 3) and line a 20 cm (8 in) shallow tart tin with baking parchment (see page 46).

Scatter 25 g (1 oz) of the sugar on a side plate. Heat a non-stick frying pan over a high heat. When hot, dip the cut side of each apricot into the sugar, then place them sugar side down in the pan. Tip in the remaining sugar from the plate. Caramelise the apricots for a few minutes, without stirring, until they become medium brown in colour on the cut side. Add 3 tablespoons of cold water to the pan and shake to combine the water with the sugar. Tip the contents of the pan gently into the lined tart tin, allowing the apricots and caramel to slide in sugar side down. Set aside.

Cream the remaining sugar and the butter together in a large bowl with an electric whisk or in a stand mixer until light and fluffy. Add the remaining ingredients and blend together with the whisk. Spoon the batter onto the apricots and smooth the top with a spatula. Bake in the oven for around 45 minutes or until a skewer inserted into the middle of the cake comes out clean. Remove from the oven with oven gloves and put a plate over the top of the tin. Flip the cake over and peel off the baking parchment. Serve warm or at room temperature with whipped cream or Saffron Custard (see page 244).

marietta's pannacotta

SERVES
8 PEOPLE

3 egg whites
600 ml (20 fl oz/2½ cups) whipping cream
75 g (2½ oz/⅓ cup) caster (superfine) sugar
finely grated zest of 1 orange
1 teaspoon vanilla extract
1 teaspoon ground cinnamon (optional)
approx. 32 raspberries (optional)

This creamy, custardy pudding made by Giancarlo's mother, Marietta, is not like the more northern Italian pannacotta that wobbles as it is served. It is more like an English posset, set firm and not turned out. Do leave the fruits out if you prefer, or use any fruits to hand such as blueberries, halved strawberries, stoned cherries, the blackberries from the Blackberry Compote (see page 68), quartered ripe apricots or figs. Use the leftover egg yolks to make the Saffron Custard on page 244.

Preheat the oven to 150°C (300°F/Gas 2). Whisk the egg whites in a large bowl until they are fluffy. Add the remaining ingredients (except the raspberries, if using) and whisk together until well combined. Pour into eight 8 cm (3 in) ramekins, then put the ramekins into a roasting tray. Divide the raspberries (if using) evenly between the ramekins. Fill the tray with cold water until it comes halfway up the ramekins. Bake the pannacottas for 50 minutes–1 hour until they are firm to the touch. Remove from the oven and leave until they are just warm and serve, or leave to cool fully and chill in the fridge. Serve them warm or chilled (they will keep in the fridge for up to 3 days) with chilled Vin Santo and the *ricciarelli* biscuits on page 71.

●

Variation: Saffron pannacotta
Instead of using the orange, vanilla and cinnamon to flavour the dessert, use a good pinch of saffron strands that have been soaked in 1 tablespoon of very hot water for 15 minutes. Add this water and the saffron strands to the egg with the rest of the ingredients.

●

chocolate & hazelnut cake

SERVES
8–10 PEOPLE

- 300 g (10½ oz/generous 2 cups) hazelnuts, blanched or with thin skins on
- 200 g (7 oz) dark (bittersweet) chocolate (minimum 70% cocoa solids), broken into pieces
- 200 g (7 oz) salted or unsalted butter, plus extra for greasing (optional)
- 6 medium eggs, separated
- 25 g (1 oz) caster (superfine) sugar
- 75 ml (2 ½ fl oz/⅓ cup) cold espresso
- 3 tablespoons Cognac
- whipped cream, to serve (optional)

Our chef friend Antonella Secciani's father used to grow two hazel trees in his garden. These trees supplied the family with hazelnuts for her mother to use for cakes such as this. Antonella brought this rich and decadent cake as a present to us one Christmas as it is gluten-free, and we asked if we could include the recipe in the book. The sugar quantity is low as Giancarlo is diabetic but the chocolate contains sugar, so the sweetness is just right.

Preheat the oven to 180°C (350°F/Gas 4). Grease a 24 cm (10 in) springform cake tin with butter, or, if you don't have a springform tin, line the base of a shallow cake tin of similar dimensions with baking parchment.

Put the hazelnuts in a roasting tray and roast for 5 minutes or until just golden brown. Remove from the oven and set aside to cool.

Put the chocolate and butter in a small saucepan over a low heat and melt together, stirring constantly. Remove from the heat as soon as the mixture is smooth and no lumps remain, and set aside. (This can also be done in a microwave.)

When the hazelnuts are cool, blitz them to a fine powder in a food processor or chop them by hand. The choice of texture is up to you – smooth or crunchy.

Whisk the egg yolks and sugar in a large bowl for 4–5 minutes until pale and fluffy. Add the hazelnuts to the bowl and whisk to combine, then pour in the espresso, Cognac and melted chocolate mixture, and whisk through.

Beat the egg whites in a spotlessly clean bowl with an electric whisk until they form stiff peaks, then fold them into the cake mixture with a large metal spoon. Pour the mixture into the cake tin. Bake for 30 minutes or until the top feels firm to the touch and doesn't wobble. If the cake wobbles, bake it for a little longer. Remove from the oven and leave to cool in the tin. Serve with whipped cream and a shot of strong espresso.

fruit salads

In Italy, a salad made from a combination of fresh fruits has been known as a *macedonia* since the 18th century. No one seems to know exactly why, but it could be something to do with Alexander the Great's Macedonian Empire being made up from diverse cultures. Here are a few of our favourite combinations that are so easy, yet taste more than the sum of their parts.

CACHI, MASCARPONE E BASILICA

persimmons, mascarpone & basil

SERVES
6 PEOPLE

4 ripe persimmons
a splash of Vin Santo or other sweet wine or brandy
handful of small basil leaves, to serve

FOR THE CREAM
200 g (7 oz/scant 1 cup) mascarpone
5 tablespoons Vin Santo, other sweet wine or brandy
1–2 tablespoons icing (confectioners') sugar

If you have ever seen bright orange, shiny globes on bare trees in late autumn or early winter in Tuscany, those are persimmons (also known as *cachi* or sharon fruit). They look like embarrassed baubles that have arrived a little early for the Christmas party. If it is a cold year they are often brought in to ripen in a warm place at home. Giancarlo buys them firm and puts them in a small basket of straw in our kitchen. He watches them daily like someone waiting for eggs to hatch. When soft and tender to the touch he slices off the top and eats them with a spoon. They are naturally sweet and good for dessert or with cheese.

Wash the persimmons in cold water. Cut off and discard the tops, and slice the flesh into 5 mm- (¼ in-) thick circles. Lay them on a serving plate and splash over the wine. Combine the ingredients for the cream and adjust the sweetness to your liking. Dollop the cream around the plate and scatter over the basil leaves. Serve straight away or chill in the fridge for 30 minutes.

strawberries with orange & lemon juice

SERVES
6 PEOPLE

juice of 1 orange
juice of 1 lemon
1–2 tablespoons mild runny
     honey, to taste
600 g (1 lb 5 oz) ripe
     strawberries, sliced
few mint leaves, to serve

Strawberries are often served with lemon juice in Italy, or a combination of lemon and orange. If you have other berries to hand, do mix them in as well. Slices of ripe nectarine make a lovely addition. If the strawberries are not sweet enough, add honey to the juices (but you may not need any).

Mix the lemon and orange juices in a bowl with the honey to taste. Arrange the strawberry slices on a large serving platter with any other berries or fruit (if using). Splash on the sweet juice and serve, or chill in the fridge for up to 3 hours. Dress with a few mint leaves just before serving.

peaches in red wine

SERVES
4–6 PEOPLE

4 large ripe peaches
     (or nectarines)
25 g (1 oz) caster
     (superfine) sugar
juice of ½ lemon
500 ml (17 fl oz/2¼ cups)
     red wine

Our friend Antonella Secciani told us of her father's favourite treat in the height of summer: if he spotted a perfectly ripe peach he would pick it from his *orto* (allotment), slice it, and drop it into his glass of red wine. After just a few minutes he would eat the peach and drink the wine.

Wash the peaches in cold water. Cut them in half and remove the stones, then cut them into 1 cm (½ in) wedges. Put them in a bowl with the sugar and lemon juice, and leave in the fridge for 15 minutes.

Divide the peach slices between 4–6 glasses and top each one with red wine. Leave in the fridge again to macerate for up to 2 hours. Encourage your guests to spear the peaches with a fork then drink the peach-flavoured wine.

RICCI & PIERI DI SIM
CAFFÉ

acknowledgements

RESTAURANTS WE LOVE

LA TANA DEI BRILLI
v.lo ciambellano 4
58024 Massa Marittima
latanadeibrilli.it

BUCA DI SANT'ANTONIO
Via della Cervia, 3
55100 Lucca
bucadisantantonio.com

TRATTORIA I BARBERI
Via Stalloreggi 10,
53100 Siena
trattoriaibarberi.it

IL DIVO, SIENA
Via Franciosa 25/29
53100 Siena
osteriadadivo.it

PORT ELLEN CLAN, LUCCA
Via del Fosso 120
55100 Lucca
portellenclan.com

**OUR FAVOURITE PLACES
TO STAY IN TUSCANY**

LA MANDRIOLA AGRITURISMO
Loc. La Mandriola
56030 Lajatico (Pisa)
agriturismolamandriola.com

PALAZZO NOBILE DI SAN DONATO
via di San Donato 6
53045 Montepulciano (Siena)
palazzosandonato.it

Thank you so much to…

At home
Our publisher, the amazing Kate Pollard, supported by lovely Kajal Mistry and the ever-patient and caring Hannah Roberts and Eila Purvis.

Helen Cathcart for your beautiful photographs as ever, and clever styling by Rosie Birkett and Juliet Baptiste-Kelly.

Laura Nickoll for her careful editing and making sense of my ideas and grammar.

Susan Pegg for her attention to detail.

Anne Hudson for creating, testing and for the fun we had working out so many recipes over the last year.

Stefano Borella for testing recipes, especially the panforte – we did it!

Angela Ruocco for translation at a minute's notice.

Designer Claire Warner and illustrator Richard Robinson for making such a stunning book.

Roger and Sheila Brocklehurst for hours of wading through Tuscan history to find the culinary gems.

Brian McLeod for his middle-of-the-night research, criticism and ideas.

Karen Courtney for being word-perfect and patient.

The Gallery girls of Gerrards Cross for looking after me – I'd be Worzel Gummidge without you lot!

In Tuscany
Antonella Secciani for teaching me the principles of Tuscan cooking.

For all your help, time and recipes, Giancarlo Barbafieri and all at Mandriola.

Ilaria Biagi and mum Elena Rosini, Fabrizio Biagi and Antonella Rossi.

Livia, Nello and Daniele for having one of my favourite places in the world and always making us feel at home.

Franca Buonamici and family for your time and kind hospitality always.

Titziana Caldesi and husband Massimo for your fabulous food and generosity.

Elizabeth Orchard, Claire and Mirko, who made us so welcome last Christmas.

about the authors

Owners of London's Caffè Caldesi, Caldesi in Campagna in Bray, and the Marylebone La Cucina Caldesi cooking school, Katie and Giancarlo Caldesi have a passion for Italian food. They have spent over 16 years teaching students at every level, and have written 10 cookbooks. Katie and Giancarlo have two children, Giorgio and Flavio.

caldesi.com

index

coffee 56–7
    coffee & ricotta shots 66–7
Cognac: coffee & ricotta
    shots 66–7
compotes: blackberry
    compote 68
courgettes
    courgette & tomato ragù
    84–5
    farro, courgette, mint &
    walnut salad 89, 91
    roasted vegetables 230
    vegetables steamed in
    paper 236–7
crab: linguine with crab
    & cream 100–1
cream
    choux buns 74–5
    choux pastry with chicken
    livers, cream & lemon
    154–5
    Florentine cake 72–3
    Grana Padano timbale 157
    hot chocolate 69
    linguine with crab
    & cream 100–1
    Marietta's pannacotta 253
    Tuscan vegetable timbales
    in a Pecorino cheese
    sauce 158–9
creamy bean soup 145, 146
crostini
    fig & mascarpone or
    ricotta crostini with honey
    64–5
    toasted bread topped with
    chicken liver pâté 119, 121
cucumber: tomato & cucumber
    salad 218–19
custard: apple cake with
    saffron custard 244

d

drinks
    coffee 56–7
    coffee & ricotta shots 66–7
    hot chocolate 69
duck ragù 177

e

eggs
    babbo's eggs 59
    Grana Padano timbale 157
    a herbed dish 86, 88
    large ravioli filled with
    spinach & an egg yolk 182–3
    Marietta's pannacotta 253
    Swiss chard & egg soup
    148–9

f

Fabrizio's hand-rolled pasta
    strands 181
farro
    farro, courgette, mint &
    walnut salad 89, 91
    farro soup with prawns 138
fennel: white cabbage, fennel
    & onions with saffron 234–5
fennel seeds: pork tenderloin
    with Flavio's Tuscan 'dust'
    206–7
fig & mascarpone or ricotta
    crostini with honey 64–5
Florentine cake 72–3
Florentine pancakes 186–7
fontina cheese: puff pastry pie
    with cheese & ham 76–7
frangipane: apricot &
    frangipane cake 250–1
fruit, candied
    aniseed biscuits 70–1
    Antonella's panforte
    246–7
fruit, preserving 50
fruit salads
    peaches in red wine 260
    persimmons, mascarpone
    & basil 259
    strawberries with orange
    & lemon juice 260

g

garlic
    battuto 29
    Giancarlo's Tuscan chicken
    with rosemary & garlic 108
    pasta with roasted
    tomatoes, chilli & garlic
    102–3
    sautéed leaves with chilli
    & garlic 227
    swordfish alla Livornese
    194
Giancarlo's cannellini beans
    223
Giancarlo's Tuscan chicken
    with rosemary & garlic 108
gnocchi 161
    chestnut & potato gnocchi
    165
    kale & ricotta gnocchi in
    sage & bacon butter 162–3
Gorgonzola: cheese & mixed
    seed cantuccini 118, 121
Grana Padano
    Grana Padano timbale 157
    Tuscan vegetable timbales
    in a Pecorino cheese sauce
    158–9

green beans: vegetables
    steamed in paper 236–7
greens, cooking 38

h

ham: puff pastry pie with
    cheese & ham 76–7
hazelnuts: chocolate &
    hazelnut cake 256–7
herbs 43
    battuto 29
    a herbed dish 86, 88
    pork tenderloin with Flavio's
    Tuscan 'dust' 206–7
    sea bass cooked in a parcel
    with Tuscan herbs 195

i

jam: plum jam 62–3

k

kale
    black kale bruschetta 86
    kale & ricotta gnocchi in
    sage & bacon butter 162–3
    kale & sausage pasta
    sauce 98–9

l

la bistecca Fiorentina 210–13
leeks
    pheasant & leek risotto 112
    potatoes & leeks or spring
    onions 224
    roasted vegetables 230
    vegetables steamed in
    paper 236–7
lemons
    chestnut pancakes filled
    with ricotta & lemon 248–9
    choux pastry with chicken
    livers, cream & lemon
    154–5
    strawberries with orange
    & lemon juice 260
lentils
    lentils with soffritto 229
    Tiziana's lentil soup 150–1
linguine with crab & cream
    100–1
liver: calf's liver with butter
    & sage 197

m

Marietta's pannacotta 253
mascarpone
    fig & mascarpone or ricotta
    crostini with honey 64–5
    mascarpone cheesecake
    alla Port Ellen clan 245
    persimmons, mascarpone
    & basil 259
meatloaf: chicken meatloaf
    202
Memmo's beef ragù 170–1
milk
    béchamel sauce 189
    Grana Padano timbale 157
    hot chocolate 69
minestrone: winter soup 142–3
mint: farro, courgette, mint
    & walnut salad 89, 91
mozzarella cheese
    courgette & tomato ragù
    84–5
    ravioli filled with tomato
    & bread stuffing in a warm
    mozzarella cream 172–3
    toasted bread with
    mozzarella & porcini
    mushrooms 120, 125
mushrooms
    porcini & chestnut
    mushroom loaf 204–5
    porcini risotto 111
    stuffed vegetables 190
    toasted bread with
    mozzarella & porcini
    mushrooms 120, 125
    Tuscan beef, porcini &
    Chianti stew 209

o

olive oil 26
    battuto 29
    toasted bread with
    tomatoes & olive oil 59, 60
olives
    rabbit in white wine 198–9
    rabbit casserole 110
onions
    fricassee of chicken with
    sage & onions 106–7
    peas, bacon & onions 220
    roasted vegetables 230
    split broad beans with fried
    onions 232
oranges: strawberries with
    orange & lemon juice 260

Tuscany by
Katie & Giancarlo Caldesi

First published in 2017
by Hardie Grant Books

Hardie Grant Books (UK)
52–54 Southwark Street
London SE1 1UN
hardiegrant.com

Hardie Grant Books (Australia)
Ground Floor, Building 1
658 Church Street
Melbourne, VIC 3121
hardiegrant.com

The moral rights of
Katie & Giancarlo Caldesi
to be identified as the authors
of this work has been asserted
by them in accordance with
the Copyright, Designs and
Patents Act 1988.

Text ©
Katie & Giancarlo Caldesi 2017
Photography ©
Helen Cathcart 2017

All rights reserved. No part
of this publication may be
reproduced, stored in a
retrieval system or transmitted
in any form by any means,
electronic, electrostatic,
magnetic tape, mechanical,
photocopying, recording
or otherwise, without the
prior written permission
of the Publisher.

British Library Cataloguing-in-
Publication Data. A catalogue
record for this book is available
from the British Library.

ISBN: 978-178488-119-1

Publisher: Kate Pollard
Senior Editor: Kajal Mistry
Editorial Assistant:
Hannah Roberts
Publishing Assistant: Eila Purvis
Design: Claire Warner Studio
Illustrator © Richard Robinson
Icons on page 57 ©
Art Shop, Yohann Berger,
Tereza Moravcová, Rohith M S,
Federico Panzano & Andrey
Vasiliev, from the Noun Project
Photography © Helen Cathcart
Prop Stylist: Linda Berlin
Copy editor: Laura Nickoll
Proofreader: Susan Pegg
Indexer: Cathy Heath
Colour Reproduction by p2d
Printed and bound in China
by 1010

10 9 8 7 6 5 4 3 2 1